Rudy Maxa's
Smart Travels in Europe

CO-AUTHORED BY

Rudy Maxa
Patty Conroy
Susan McNally
Laura Mancuso

A COMPANION TO THE PUBLIC TELEVISION SERIES

SMART TRAVELS—EUROPE WITH RUDY MAXA

PRODUCED BY SMALL WORLD PRODUCTIONS, INC., AND KCTS/SEATTLE

ISBN 1-57959-518-9

FIRST PUBLISHED BY SMALL WORLD PRODUCTIONS, INC.

BAY BOOKS IS AN IMPRINT OF BAY/SOMA PUBLISHING, INC.,
555 DE HARO STREET, #220, SAN FRANCISCO, CA 94107.

BOOK DESIGN	Lisa Moore
COVER DESIGN	Derek Yee
PHOTOGRAPHER	Tom Speer Photographs are frame-captures from HDTV video
EDITORS	Laura Mancuso Ann Conroy John Givens
COPY EDITOR	Sarah Pirch

Library of Congress Cataloging-in-Publication Data is available from the publisher.

Several articles in this book were originally published in Rudy Maxa's Traveler Newsletter. They are reprinted here with permission.

The authors and the publishers have done their best to ensure the accuracy of information in Smart Travels.TV, a companion book to the public television series; however, they can accept no responsibility for any loss, injury or inconvenience sustained by any traveler as a result of information or advice contained in this book. Please write with your comments, suggestions, updates and corrections. Writers of the best letters will receive a free video of a Smart Travels episode.

Small World Travel Videos

$24.95 each – any 5 for $99.95

Smart Travels
Europe with Rudy Maxa

- **Naples & the Amalfi Coast/Rome** (2 EPISODES–60 MINUTES)
- **Venice/Genoa & the Italian Riviera** (2 EPISODES–60 MINUTES)
- **Florence/Italian Hill Towns** (2 EPISODES–60 MINUTES)
- **Provence/Paris** (2 EPISODES–60 MINUTES)
- **London/Out of London** (2 EPISODES–60 MINUTES)
- **Belgium/Netherlands/Denmark** (3 EPISODES–90 MINUTES)

Travels in Europe
with Rick Steves

4 award-winning series/25 video tapes! INCLUDING:
Austria, Belgium, Eastern Europe, Egypt, France, Germany, Great Britain, Greece, Holland, Ireland, Israel, Italy, Luxembourg, Portugal, Scandinavia, Spain, Switzerland, Turkey

Travels in Mexico & the Caribbean
with Shari Belafonte

- **Martinique, St. Kitts & Antigua**
- **Puerto Rico & the U.S. Virgin Islands**
- **Jamaica, Miami & the Bahamas**
- **Mexico City & Guadalajara**
- **Cuernavaca & Oaxaca**
- **Merida, Cancun & Belize**

America's Historic Trails
with Tom Bodett

- **The Old Post Road: New York to Boston**
- **The Great Wagon Road & the Wilderness Road: Philadelphia to Kentucky**
- **New Orleans & the Natchez Trace**
- **The Mormon Trail & the California Trail**
- **The Yukon Gold Rush Trail: Seattle and Alaska**
- **California's Mission Trail & New Mexico's El Camino Real**

VISIT US ONLINE: **www.smarttravels.tv**
ORDERS: **1.800.866.7425**
VISA, MC, AMEX, DISCOVER

SHIPPING & HANDLING $4.00
SEND CHECKS TO:

SMALL WORLD PRODUCTIONS, INC.
P.O. BOX 28369
SEATTLE, WA 98118-8369

▪ ▪ ▪ ▪ Contents

Introduction

Travel and Technology BY RUDY MAXA 9

Destinations

London 15

Out of London 27

Copenhagen and Denmark 33

Amsterdam and The Netherlands 41

Belgium 51

Paris 59

Provence 67

Venice 77

Italian Riviera 85

Hill Towns of Tuscany and Umbria 93

Florence 101

Rome 109

Naples and the Amalfi Coast 117

Travel Tips and Lessons Learned BY RUDY MAXA

Phoning Home From Abroad 125

Medical Emergencies Abroad:
Don't Leave Home Until You Read This! 129

Mi Casa, Su Casa: Swapping Homes with a Stranger Overseas–
Would You Dare? 133

Smart Sites 137

About the Producers of Smart Travels

Biographies 140

Producers' Acknowledgments 143

Index 149

▨ ▨ ▨ ■ Introduction

TRAVEL AND TECHNOLOGY:
High-Tech Prep and Digital Devices Are Keys to
Smart Travels in Century 21

By Rudy Maxa

THE FIRST TIME I VISITED ST. PETERSBURG, RUSSIA, it was called Leningrad, and Russia was still the Soviet Union. I arrived on short notice with a thin guidebook in my pocket and a list of three local names. The names were friends of friends who, I was assured, would introduce me to the city.

When I went for a walk shortly after checking into my hotel, KGB agents searched and burgled my room. I think they call it "tossing a room" in spy jargon. How did I know it was the work of the KGB? The hotel's Swedish-born general manager told me; in fact, he seemed bemused that I was upset. The intruders took my copy of John le Carré's novel *Russia House*, my daybook and that slip of paper with the names and phone numbers of local contacts. I didn't understand why they left behind the $2,000 in $100 bills I'd brought along as spending money.

"Because there were two of them," explained William Colby, the former head of the CIA, when I told him about my experience during a flight to Tokyo a few days later. (We just happened to be seated next to each other. Coincidence? I think not!) "Neither guy trusted the other," he said, "to keep the theft of so much money a secret."

Well, now, that was interesting.

At the time, of course, I was grateful to still have my money. But I was upset at the loss of my list of local contacts because my guidebook—like many guidebooks in the '80s dealing with the Soviet Union—was hopelessly out of date and short on details.

Today, I would not be without resources. I'd use a modem-equipped laptop, dial a local number, and find up-to-date information on almost anything I needed to know. Because traveling today is very different than before.

I have a hard time sitting still. My father was a U.S. Army officer, and when I was a kid, my family moved every year or so. I grew up everywhere from Huntsville, Alabama, to Heidelberg, Germany. When I graduated from college and began my life as a journalist at the *Washington Post*, I worked overtime trying to think up out-of-town story ideas.

The idea was to travel.

Anywhere.

After more than 12 years at the Post as an investigative reporter, magazine writer and personalities columnist, I joined the monthly city magazine *Washingtonian*. Now, here was a challenge: How to snare overseas assignments while working for a very local magazine. I managed. A big musical called *Les Miserables* was all the rage in London; it would make its North American debut at the Kennedy Center in Washington. Hadn't I better get over to London to see the show? And then visit Paris to interview the two men behind the musical's words and lyrics so *Washingtonian* would have a splashy article timed with the show's opening?

You bet.

Remember the residents of the tiny island of Bikini way out in the middle of the Pacific Ocean in the Marshall Islands? We'd displaced the Bikinians in order to test the atom bomb during World War II. Since then, they hadn't been able to return home because their island was contaminated by radiation. They'd become wards of Uncle Sam. The federal government sent them surplus food, and a people accustomed to eating fresh fish and fruit saw their health deteriorate on a distinctly nonisland diet of canned ham and other Western staples. Wouldn't an article on the legacy of nuclear testing and the effect of a distant welfare state run by Washington bureaucrats be in order? Hadn't I best get over to Majuro quickly?

You get the picture.

Eventually, the business of travel began taking over my professional life. When J.J. Yore, a producer from public radio's evening business show, *Marketplace*, called in 1990 to ask me to contribute regular political commentary, I declined the honor. Instead, I suggested a regular segment on consumer travel issues. My friend Peter Greenberg was then writing a similar syndicated column for the *Los Angeles Times* called *The Savvy Traveler*. I thought that was a catchy name, and with his permission, I borrowed it for use on the radio. I began writing on consumer travel issues for *Worth* magazine and, later, *Forbes* and *Men's Journal*, among others.

Shortly after *Savvy Traveler*® became a one-hour, coast-to-coast show on public radio in 1997, I began writing a weekly travel column for MSNBC.com. And then SMALL WORLD PRODUCTIONS—which had produced 10 years' worth of travel shows about Europe as well as Mexico and the Caribbean—gave me the opportunity to host public television's first high-definition series, **Smart Travels with Rudy Maxa**.

It was time to reflect. SMALL WORLD had done dozens of shows about Europe. What, I wondered, was "new" about travel?

In my opinion, the biggest change in travel since the invention of the jet engine is the high-tech revolution. In the last six years, learning about a destination, how to get there and what to do once you've arrived has become a breeze. We tap into data banks with a flurry of fingers over a computer keyboard. We compare airline, hotel and rental car prices and pit low-cost providers against each other without having to pick up a phone and listen to recordings telling us all agents are temporarily busy.

Using web-enabled cell phones, we can find the location of the nearest ATM or gas station almost anywhere in the world. We make and receive phone calls as easily in Paris as in our hometown. Hand-held global positioning devices coordinate with satellites to tell us exactly where we are should we get lost.

Want to check out which operas are coming up just about anywhere from Amsterdam to Sydney to Pretoria to Vienna? Click onto **www.operahouse.com**, a multilingual web site that tracks the goings-on at more than 700 opera houses and festivals around the globe. Often, you can click on a link to buy tickets to an opera that strikes your fancy. Want to know how many U.S. dollars 1,300,000 Italian lire represents? There are hundreds of sites that convert currencies in a few seconds—you'll find a link to a currency converter at **www.expedia.com**, for example. Whether it's a Tokyo subway schedule (**www.tokyometro.go.jp/e-home/index-e.html**) or a menu of spa treatments at a luxury resort in India (**www.oberoihotels.com**), information that took days to find just a few years ago is now only a few computer mouse clicks away.

And whether you travel with a backpack, frequent Internet cafes and stay in hostels, or whether you carry a cell phone, laptop and personal digital assistant and stay at five-star hotels, you're traveling differently than ever before. Ours, after all, is the world's first Techno-Travel Generation.

This is good. Even if you journey to escape the rush of life, to listen to your soul and wander down unmapped dirt roads, technology is your friend. After all, you can turn off that cell phone, laptop and personal digital assistant. But if you need them, they're there.

Sometimes they can bring unexpected pleasure.

I remember changing planes at Frankfurt's airport en route to joining the *Smart Travels* crew for filming in Venice. I'd just bought a dual-band cell phone that worked in the United States as well as in countries that use the GSM (Global System for Mobile Communications) standard, as most European countries do. I was startled when it first rang in my pocket, because I'd never received a cell phone call overseas.

It was my high-school-age son calling from Washington, D.C., to tell me he'd scored a goal in a lacrosse game that afternoon. When I rang off, I stood dumbfounded in the gate area of my connecting flight. There I was in faraway Germany, hearing from my son as effortlessly as if I'd been home in Washington. It probably wasn't incredible to him—his generation is accustomed to instantaneous communication—but for those of us who remember life before the invention of answering machines and phones without wires, receiving a transatlantic call on a little phone in your pocket is nothing short of miraculous.

During the months the **Smart Travels** crew and I taped in Europe, we were constantly reminded of how technology can make travel easier. Need more cash? No need to stand in line at an American Express office to write a check against a credit card, as I once did regularly. Slip that ATM card from your hometown bank into an automatic teller machine in downtown Amsterdam and out slides Dutch money (guilders) from your checking account. And at a pretty favorable exchange rate, too.

The crew and I worked at a brisk pace. Watching our shows about, say, Tuscany or Provence, I hope you feel the serenity of the places we visited. And while we were never oblivious to the natural beauty of those charming places or the kindness of locals, "serene" wouldn't necessarily be the adjective I'd use to describe the days and nights we spent shooting.

Inclement weather, traffic jams, fickle museum hours, cranky bureaucrats, lost luggage and other forces sometimes conspired to tangle our schedule. I remember one afternoon when we were running late for a lunch with the Castello Banfi wine folks in Tuscany. Once upon a time not very long ago, we would have been even later. That's because we would have had to pull our car over to the side of the road, search out a public phone, hope we had enough coins or the correct phone card, and pray we could figure out the local dialing code in order to make our apologies.

Instead, as we zipped along in our Avis car, we simply pulled out a cell phone, called our contact and said we'd be arriving an hour late.

No problemo.

Touring Genoa, we had the expert help of Roberto Stubinski, a local doctor who knew one of my best friends from my hometown of Washington. Roberto kindly took time off work to show us around his hometown. We traveled in a van while he zipped around Genoa and the hill towns of the Italian Riviera on a motorbike with his girlfriend, Maria. We stayed in touch using cell phones, which is how we found Roberto waiting for us at a great, hole-in-the-wall pizza place across the street from Genoa's Port Antico. And later, at a seafood restaurant popular with locals that was perched on a cliff overlooking the water outside Camogli.

Frankly, without those phones, we probably would have spent hours trying to rendezvous.

You don't have to carry an array of electronic devices to qualify as a Techno-Traveler. In fact, if you do enough advance planning, you'll do just fine on the road with nothing but a smile and credit or ATM card. The odds are pretty good that if you use the Internet to research a trip before you leave, you'll enjoy a richer experience.

Not only is there a vast world of information on places, there are all kinds of message boards where fellow travelers post their experiences. So if you're not sure whether a specific cruise ship fits your personality or if a resort is really as wonderful as its brochure or web site promises, there's usually a place you can look to read the candid remarks of someone who went before you.

So my advice to anyone embarking on a trip to a new place is to take a leisurely evening and surf the web. Using different search engines such as **www.google.com**, **www.yahoo.com** and **www.altavista.com**, type in keywords such as "Amalfi and wine" and see what comes up. It won't be difficult to find an array of material on places, hotels, bike routes, and so on. You can access guidebooks by going to **www.lonelyplanet.com**, **www.frommers.com** or **www.fodors.com**, but sometimes information can be outdated if the reporting is by folks who visited sites a year earlier.

Don't forget to browse newspapers published in the place you're planning to visit. Almost every newspaper has a web site, and that's a great place to find out what's going on in a destination at any given time. (Start with **www.mediainfo.com** and **www.newsdirectory.com**.) Magazines including Time Out (**www.timeout.com**) offer all kinds of information on specific cities. Time Out's site delivers fresh information on where to shop, what's on and where to eat in more than two dozen major cities around the world.

Convention and visitors' bureaus, too, have web sites with up-to-the-minute information. Check the Tourism Offices Worldwide Directory at **www.towd.com** for hyperlinks to more than 1,500 offices of folks who would love to send you brochures or answer questions about their destinations.

Then there are web sites begun by people just wild about particular places, such as **www.bparis.com**, operated by an American ex-pat, Karen Fawcett, who wanted to share her love of Paris with the rest of the world. It's developed into a sophisticated site.

What will the future hold? More of the same, except bigger, better and faster. Late one afternoon in the winter of 2000, I was driving north toward Los Angeles along the San Diego Freeway in southern California with my girlfriend. We had a few hours to kill and wanted to catch a certain movie we'd read about. As neither of us knew the area, we had no idea which of the many beachside communities might have movie theaters, let alone which movies were playing in them at what time.

"Hang on," said Lesley, "I'll find out."

She dialed 800-555-TELL on her cell phone, worked her way through a series of menus by speaking commands, and within minutes we were movie-bound.

Just as I'd been amazed at my son's ability to reach out from Washington, D.C., and talk to me while I stood in a German airport, so, too, was I astounded that Lesley could pinpoint any movie anywhere in the country as we sped along a freeway.

Following computer prompts, she'd said the name of the movie, the name of the town and then the approximate show time we wanted. Within seconds, she'd learned the address of the theater showing the film and that day's show times. She also could have bought the tickets by phone if she'd so desired. If she'd had a laptop with a wireless modem, she could have done the same thing by going to **www.tellme.com**.

Via computer or phone, you can tap into the Tellme web site and receive reviews of restaurants, movie information around the United States, driving directions, ski reports, sports scores, stock quotes and even your horoscope. If you missed an episode of your favorite soap opera, Tellme will fill you in if you ask.

It's only a matter of time until similar information services are available around the world.

We can only begin to imagine what tomorrow's Techno-Travelers will be able to accomplish. I think the bottom line will be this: Travelers will have more time to do what they travel for, whether it's to linger in a museum in Rome, people-watch over an espresso at a Parisian café or catch a concert in Copenhagen.

Certainly, traveling is as much about the journey as the destination, and there will still be adventures involved in getting somewhere. A survey conducted on the eve of the new millennium revealed that most Americans believe that by the next millennium, scientists will have invented a way to instantly teleport us around the globe. We'll be able to step into a machine in Pittsburgh, choose "Athens, Greece," and moments later, we'll find ourselves walking around an ancient temple.

But I have faith that every once in a while, someone's luggage will wind up in Athens, Georgia. Or because of adverse atmospheric conditions, their trip will be delayed.

Just a word of advice: Never, ever leave $2,000 in $100 bills in an unattended hotel room. Because all the technology in the world can't replace cash. And maybe there won't be two of 'em should your room ever get tossed by a hostile intelligence agency.

London

Tourism Web Site: www.londontown.com

Tourist Office: Greenwich Tourist Information Centre
Pepys House
2 Cutty Sark Gardens
Greenwich, SE10,
Tel: 020-8858-6376
Rail: Greenwich
Underground: North Greenwich
Open daily 10 a.m.–5 p.m. Apr.–Sept.; otherwise open with
reduced hours

How can you resist a country that gave us Mother Goose, Shakespeare, Henry VIII and the Beatles? In no small way, England has left its imprint on the world, and London is the country's nerve center. During your visit, you'll notice that traditional London, with its royalty and formal air, is alive and well, but you'll also see hints of an increasingly unified Europe and a cutting-edge arts scene like no other.

The city is a drama in real life, where imperial history is the backdrop and modern business and art provide the action. Though many British traditions continue to thrive here, the hip youth culture of Brit pop and techno are sweeping the world. And that is the nature of London—trendsetting, surprising and always a force to be reckoned with.

To really know London, you'll want to visit the sites and museums for which the city is known. You'll find, however, that it's equally satisfying to visit this city on a personal level, seeking out neighborhoods that appeal to you and engage your imagination. Browse in bookshops, sample pubs and chat up the locals. London has an endless amount of diversity, and discovering it on your own is half the fun.

Trafalgar Square
This square, the center of London, is dedicated to Admiral Lord Nelson, one of England's great military heroes. Nelson died defeating Napoleon at the Battle of Trafalgar in 1805, a time during which the British navy dominated the seas.

Thames River
Stand on the banks of the Thames and you can gaze down at a waterway that has been the lifeblood of London since ancient Roman times. For more than 2,000 years, this river has borne witness to London's remarkable history.

Tower of London
www.tower-of-london.co.uk

The medieval Tower of London, which has served as a royal palace, a fortress, a prison and a treasury, presides over the Thames. William the Conqueror constructed the oldest part of the tower a thousand years ago to keep control over London's native Saxon population.

Visitors seem to thrive on the Tower of London's gory history. After all, this is where King Richard III had his henchmen kill two young princes, Henry VIII had two of his wives executed on the Tower Green and Sir Thomas More and Lady Jane Grey both met their deaths. Today the tower serves a less gruesome purpose—it holds England's Armories and the Crown Jewels.

Buckingham Palace
www.royal.gov.uk/palaces

You want tradition, you got it. Located midway between Parliament and Hyde Park, Buckingham Palace stands at solemn attention and is the official residence of the queen. Buckingham became a royal residence in the mid-18th century when King George II needed room for his 15 children. Today, the palace is most famous for its daily changing-of-the-guard ceremony, a not-to-be-missed example of British pageantry. You can see the ceremony daily at 11:30 May through August and on even-numbered days September through April.

St. Paul's Cathedral
www.stpauls.co.uk

After the great London fire devastated medieval St. Paul's cathedral in 1666, church authorities brought in famed architect Christopher Wren to rebuild it. The Protestant church commissioners initially disapproved of Wren's inventive ideas. They thought his plan for a great Italian-style dome was too reminiscent of Rome. Eventually they reached a compromise and the architect succeeded in creating one of the most awe-inspiring sights in London. The cathedral's dome, one of the largest in the world, dominates London's skyline.

British Airways London Eye
www.british-airways.com/londoneye

This is definitely the hottest new place to get a bird's-eye view of the city. Taller than the Statue of Liberty, the "Eye" is the largest (450 ft. high and 1,600 tons!) observation wheel of its kind ever built. The wheel was built as part of a national celebration to ring in the 21st century.

The Tube

SMART TIP

The London Underground or "tube" is the fastest and easiest way to get around the city. Tube stations are marked with a distinctive red circle and blue crossbar. The system is well organized and simple to use. Pick the station you want from the diagram—each color represents a different line. Follow the colored band to see how many stops are between you and your destination, and off you go. You can buy tickets for the Underground in vending machines or at a ticket office.

THE **LONDON EYE** WAS BUILT TO USHER IN THE NEW MILLENNIUM.
IT OFFERS SPECTACULAR VIEWS OF THE HOUSES OF PARLIAMENT
AND THE THAMES RIVER.

ADDRESSES OF NOTE

221b Baker Street

This is the address made famous by Sherlock Holmes. Mystery writer Sir Arthur Conan Doyle created the investigator and gave him this fictional address. The site has no real connection to Holmes or Conan Doyle but is fun to visit all the same.

3 Abbey Road

If you're a Beatles fan, this may be one of your first stops. You can walk the crosswalk that John, Paul, George and Ringo traversed on the cover of their album of the same name. The Beatles recorded most of their work in Abbey Road Studio up the street.

48 Doughty Street

This is where Charles Dickens lived for three of his most productive years. Residing here, he wrote *Oliver Twist* and *Nicholas Nickleby*. Though Dickens had several homes in London during his lifetime, this is the only one that remains.

The Tate Modern
www.tate.org.uk

The Tate Modern is housed in the former Bankside power station. For nearly 20 years, this building provided electricity for London. Today, it's electrifying the British art scene with its displays of international modern art from 1900 to the present. You'll see works by some of the world's most inventive contemporary artists, such as Dorothy Cross and Susan Hiller. You'll also marvel at familiar 20th-century masters. Pablo Picasso's *Weeping Woman* is a startling portrait inspired by his relationship with photographer Dora Maar. Picasso's originality and virtuosity set the art world on fire. Salvador Dali's meticulous canvases are unnerving in their surreal imagery. And Andy Warhol's pop art is always eye-catching.

Covent Garden/West End
www.coventgardenlife.com

The range of theatrical entertainment in London is astonishing. Despite their reserved reputation, the British harbor a deep passion for the theater. Covent Garden and the West End neighborhoods glitter with ornate show palaces and flashy marquees. At any given time, you can pick from a dozen plays, and with so much variety you can be sure there's something for everyone. Tickets for London productions are generally less expensive than on Broadway and you'll usually find world-famous performers like Vanessa Redgrave, Richard Harris or Peter O'Toole.

FROM RUDY MAXA'S TRAVELER NEWSLETTER

On Stage in London:
The ins and outs of getting tickets and what's on

London has always been synonymous with live theater. Maybe it's tradition— London was hometown to Shakespeare, Shaw and Marlowe, after all. Maybe it's the popularity of American theater tours to the city. Whatever the reason, twice as many Broadway-caliber shows are now on stage in London (70, to be exact) as on Broadway.

No trip to London is complete without sampling the local theater scene.

Ticket Prices

London theater tickets have always cost less than those in the United States, though the difference is diminishing. Shows in the West End—the English equivalent of Broadway—can start as low as $15 and go up to as much as $65 for the bestseats at the most expensive shows. That's still cheaper than New York, where Broadway shows often peak at close to $100. On my last trip, for example, tickets for *Phantom of the Opera* started at $20 and went up to $65 in London. Tickets to London's "Fringe Theaters" (similar to our "Off-Broadway") ranged from $5 to $16, with most seats costing about $8.

Like New York, London has a half-price ticket outlet. But unlike the one near Times Square, standing in line isn't part of the experience. The booth, located in Leicester Square just off Piccadilly Circus, sells tickets (four maximum) for that day's matinee and evening performances at half price plus a $3 handling fee. Tickets are available for almost all the West End shows with the exception of a half-dozen or so blockbusters such as *Phantom* and specialty shows such as *The Mousetrap*. The complete list is posted in the window. But don't be fooled: In Leicester Square, there are now about a dozen imitation half-price outlets where you'll pay more for a ticket than at the box office. The real outlet is located in a separate building in a park-like area. For a picture of the building, go to its web site at **www.rap.clara.net/half**.

Another little-known tip for saving money: Senior citizens (60 and older) can buy unsold seats at half price on the day of the performance at any London box office. The time the tickets go on sale varies from theater to theater—as early as noon or as late as an hour before curtain.

London Differences

Not all the "West End Theaters" are in the West End, any more than all Broadway theaters are on Broadway. Along with the 70 major shows, an astounding 100 fringe shows are in production currently.

If you want orchestra seats (main floor), ask for "stalls." Balcony seats are called "dress circle." Check your ticket carefully. Evening performances can start at 7 p.m. or as late as 8:30 p.m. It's common to see Americans arriving an hour late for performances.

Unlike in the States, where matinees run on Wednesdays and weekends only, London theaters have matinees every day except Mondays. So if you want to see more shows than you have days in London, catch matinees. But once again, beware of curtain times. Matinees begin as early as 2 p.m. or as late as 5 p.m.

Theaters offer the large "souvenir" programs just as in the United States, as well as the smaller Playbill. In London, you'll have to pay for the Playbill that's free on this side of the Atlantic. But on the plus side, ice cream vendors walk down aisles selling sundaes and ice cream bars near the stage during intermission. Yes, you can eat them at your seat—it is an English tradition! Or you can order a drink to be waiting for you at intermission in theater bars. You prepay, and your order with your receipt awaits you at the right time. It's a great way to avoid lines.

What Should I See?

Choosing a show can be difficult. First, get a free London Theater Guide found in every theater lobby, ticket office and elsewhere. Published every other Monday, it contains everything you need to know about the major London shows: what's playing, who's starring, prices, performance times, theater address, nearby tube (subway) stops, phone number and length of shows. Another suggestion (especially if you want to see fringe theater) is to buy a copy of the weekly entertainment magazine, *Time Out*.

One thing's for sure: There's a play or musical to suit every taste.

It's Showtime!

Note: For tickets, see **www.albemarle-london.com** to learn what's playing and to see reviews and seating charts. To reserve seats from the United States, contact Global Tickets at 800-223-6108 or 800-669-8687.

Where the Theater is the Star: Summer shows at Regent Park (with dinner available also) are wonderful outdoor theater and, of course, the biggest star of them all is the newly remodeled, newly reopened Royal Opera House. The ROH (as Londoners call it) is spectacular. Check the schedule of ballet and opera. And above all, have dinner before the performance at one of its two newly designed dining rooms.

The British Museum
www.thebritishmuseum.ac.uk

This museum is considered to have one of the most comprehensive collections of art and artifacts in the world. During a single visit, you can gaze on vast treasures taken from Egyptian royal tombs and the legendary Black Obelisk. You might also track down the Rosetta Stone, the ancient slab that provided the key to deciphering hieroglyphs, and the Elgin Marbles, taken from the Parthenon in Athens. The British Museum's collection is so vast that it's impossible to see all its treasures in a day. Use a museum guide to decide what you want to see ahead of time and plan accordingly.

The Science Museum
www.nmsi.ac.uk

As the birthplace of the Industrial Revolution, 19th-century England hurtled mankind headlong into the age of technical efficiency. London's Science Museum contains more than 10,000 exhibits that show how science has shaped the modern world. In the **Space Gallery**, you can delve into how satellites and rockets work, and speculate about the future of space exploration. Because science is constantly evolving, the museum's curators keep up with new discoveries by regularly introducing innovative displays. The **Who Am I?** exhibit explores everyone's favorite subject—ourselves. It ponders such questions as: What makes us different from other animals? And what does DNA reveal about our genetic history? **Digitopolis** looks at the implications of digital technology today and for the future.

Houses of Parliament
www.parliament.uk

London's Houses of Parliament were originally built more than 1,000 years ago. In 1066, the Palace of Westminster became the home of William the Conqueror and his court and was the main residence of English kings for the next four centuries, until the time of Henry VIII. Virtually all of the structure was destroyed in a London fire in 1834. The present building, a Victorian masterpiece, was built in the late 18th century for the specific purpose of housing Parliament. The two architects who designed the building

THE CURRENT SITE OF THE HOUSES OF PARLIAMENT ON THE BANKS OF THE THAMES AT WESTMINSTER HAS BEEN THE SEAT OF GOVERNMENT IN ENGLAND FOR MORE THAN 500 YEARS.

are said to have suffered nervous breakdowns as a result of overwork and stress. The clock tower on the eastern end of the Houses of Parliament has become the symbol of London and has become universally known as **Big Ben**. Weighing 13 tons, the bell was hauled through the city by 16 horses.

Harrods
www.harrods.com

This department store is a London institution. Harrods sells an incredible range of merchandise, including food. The store's motto is, "*Everything for everyone everywhere.*"

Hyde Park

Hyde Park is the London equivalent to New York's Central Park. The verdant span covers two miles from **Speaker's Corner** to exclusive neighborhoods like **Kensington** and **Chelsea**. King Henry VIII seized the property from the church because he wanted more hunting grounds. Today, the park offers Londoners an escape from frenetic city life. Speaker's Corner has traditionally been a forum for political activists and colorful characters, though now it seems dominated by religious extremists. The park is divided in two by **Serpentine Lake**. Four fountains adorn the upper section of the park in front of an Italianate summer house that was designed by Christopher Wren. If you make it to the south end, take a look at the famed **Royal Albert Hall**, London's splendid glass-domed concert hall.

Madame Tussaud's Waxworks
www.madame-tussauds.com

The wax museum is by far one of London's most entertaining attractions. The lines are usually long but it's worth the wait. The museum is like a big wax amusement park where you can walk right up to life-size models of the world's most famous people, including George Washington, JFK and Mel Gibson. Madame Tussaud learned her craft in France taking death masks from the guillotined heads of Louis XVI and Marie Antoinette.

If you liked the gory history the Tower of London had to offer, don't miss the terrifying **Chamber of Horrors**.

Dulwich Picture Gallery
www.dulwichpicturegallery.org.uk

Tucked away in the picturesque neighborhood of Dulwich Village, the picture gallery is one of London's hidden gems. England's oldest public art gallery, the Dulwich Picture Gallery houses an outstanding collection of works by Rubens, Van Dyck, Rembrandt and England's own Gainsborough. The gallery owes its existence to Stanislaus II, the former King of Poland and paramour of Catherine the Great. After commissioning a London art dealer to build a collection for a gallery in Warsaw, Stanislaus abdicated and left the collection unpaid for. It was eventually given to Dulwich College.

SMART DINING

Most visitors don't think of London as being famous for its high cuisine, but over the past several decades, the city has lived down this reputation. England's revolution in eating is partly due to a growing demand for good restaurants and the fact that London is home to immigrants from all over the world. Today, the sheer variety of choices can be almost overwhelming. You can sample food from the Caribbean to Africa to Asia, not to mention nearly every country in Europe.

When I'm here, I never miss a chance to have Indian food. London boasts the best Indian food outside of India. Years of British colonial domination of India brought many Indians to London and with them some exotic family recipes. The **Tamarind Restaurant** (20/22 Queen Street) is one of my favorites. Located in London's Mayfair district, it serves up enticing North Indian–style dishes.

FROM RUDY MAXA'S TRAVELER NEWSLETTER

The Hot Way to Escape a London Winter
Taking off the chilly edge by taking afternoon tea

The ideal way to escape the damp chill of winter is to partake in the centuries-old custom of afternoon tea. And nowhere is tea done better than in London.

It's a pleasant and civilized way to revive oneself, as well, and a relatively inexpensive way to experience some of the old establishment, upper-crust hotels without having to check in. Tea can substitute for a meal, too. It's easy to pass up lunch when you know that in the middle of the afternoon you'll be enjoying finger sandwiches, scones and pastries. Or you may opt for a seating closer to 5 p.m. and enjoy the more substantial high tea, which began originally as dinner for working-class families on tight food budgets. With its additional plates of smoked or poached salmon salad, Stilton cheese tart or scrambled eggs, high tea can still qualify as a meal.

My friend Olwen Woodier takes afternoon tea every day she can on her frequent trips to London. She says the ritual is fully ingrained in her British psyche, and she highly recommends five leading hotels.

Claridge's: Considered one of London's most gracious hotels, Claridge's is sometimes called the "resort of kings and princes" because so many visiting royals stay there. Afternoon tea is held in the Reading Room, where art deco links arms with Elizabethan antiques. Tea begins with three-tiered plates holding dainty sandwiches filled with smoked salmon, chicken, ham and cucumber and cream cheese. Tiny cheese-filled puff pastries and apple-raisin scones are so moist the bowls of Devonshire clotted cream and strawberry preserves seem almost unnecessary. Miniature cakes and pastries are scrumptious morsels of mocha-flavored chocolate and lemon meringue. Pots of tea hold fragrant Darjeeling, sweet chamomile or your favorite flavor.

Brown's: Comfortable elegance reigns here, and it's easy to relax in deep armchairs and couches in one of the wood-paneled lounges. The headwaiter recites an impressive list of teas before bringing a three-tiered plate holding finger sandwiches, including one with a delicious, if unusual, sardine filling. Miniature soft-crust rolls are filled with egg and watercress. Scones studded with raisins and served with rich clotted cream and preserves arrive at the same time as the tiny lemon meringue tarts and other pastries. Fresh raspberries and strawberries complete the tray. Just when the repast seems over, the waiter sets down a large silver tray bearing Victoria sandwich cake and fruitcake.

The Ritz: Because of scheduled sittings at 3:30 and 5 p.m., reservations—as far as six weeks in advance during prime tourist weeks—are essential. Afternoon tea is served in the Palm Court. This elevated, open room adjoining the lobby is surrounded with marble columns and illuminated by a domed Victorian skylight. Seating here is traditional dining style with damask-clad chairs encircling round tables. Lapsang Souchong or another selection of tea is served with finger sandwiches containing interesting combinations of cucumber and anchovy, smoked turkey and sweet mustard and cottage cheese with carrot and hazelnuts. Scones are followed by a selection of pastries and miniature cakes. Dress up, as casual tourist attire is discouraged.

The Dorchester: The hotel du choix of the British royals ever since it was built in 1931, the Dorchester has also become the home-away-from-home for many American celebrities. Tea is served in The Promenade that runs the entire length of the ground floor. Italian marble covers the vast floor, and panels of Delft-style tiles decorate the walls. Whether you sink into the deep couches or sit on comfortable banquettes, you'll recognize famous faces passing through the lobby. Even though it may be difficult to tear your eyes away, the sandwiches, scones, pastries and cakes are also worthy of your attention. The Dorchester just won the Top Afternoon Tea award for the London area based on the quality of tea, refreshments, service, china and decor.

The Athenaeum: This boutique, luxury hotel offers tea in an anteroom that lets you order specifically what you want, perfect for a lighter (and less expensive) afternoon. A small box with a button on your table silently summons a server should you require another dollop of clotted cream. Watch for everyone from Claudia Schiffer to Joan Collins at nearby tables.

Spots for Tea
When in London, do not dial the country code (44), but add a zero in front of the new, downtown London prefix of "207."

Claridge's
Brook Street, Mayfair W1A2JQ
Tel: (44) 207-629-8860
Reservations: (44) 207-409-6229
www.savoy-group.co.uk
Cost: weekdays, $27; with champagne, $32
weekends, $39; with champagne, $43

Brown's Hotel
29-34 Albemarle Street
Mayfair W1X4BP
Tel: (44) 207-493-6020
E-mail: tea@brownshotel.com
Cost: $30; with champagne, $39

The Ritz
150 Piccadilly, London W1J9BR
Tel: (44) 207-493-8181
www.theritzhotel.co.uk/tea
Cost: $39 (champagne is not served with afternoon tea)

The Dorchester Hotel
Park Lane, London W1A2HJ
Tel: (44) 207-629-8888
E-mail: info@dorchesterhotel.com
Cost: $34; with champagne, $47
High tea: $41

The Athenaeum Hotel & Apartments
116 Piccadilly, London W1J 7BJ
Tel: (44) 207-499-3464
E-mail: info@athenaeumhotel.com
Cost: $22–$25

■ ■ ■

TOWER BRIDGE SPANS THE THAMES FROM THE TOWER OF LONDON AND THE DOCKSIDE COMPLEX TO THE NEW GLOBE THEATRE.

SMART LODGING

For an oasis of calm and elegance in the middle of fast-paced London, you can stay at the **Athenaeum Hotel**. Independently run, the Athenaeum has the distinctive touches and attention to detail of a really fine hotel, but maintains a cozy, friendly feel. The Athenaeum's elegant sitting room is an ideal place to savor the English ritual of afternoon tea. Unlike most of the other fine hotels, where there is a set price for afternoon tea, here you can choose from a range of options from a basic pot of tea to a full high tea, complete with tempting arrays of pastries. **www.athenaeumhotel.com**

For other listings, check **www.london.hotelguide.net**.

Out of London

Tourism Web Site: www.travelbritain.org

Tourist Office: Oxford Tourist Information Centre
The Old School
Gloucester Green
Oxford OX1 2DA
www.oxford.gov.uk/tourism

The country outside of London echoes with storybook images. Mythic castles, ruined abbeys and prehistoric monuments dot the countryside, entwining history with literary imagination. To visitors it seems as though a garden maze or majestic manor lies around each bend.

Like a trip through the looking glass, the English countryside brings childhood images to life. These are the sights that inspired luminaries like William Wordsworth, Geoffrey Chaucer and Thomas Hardy. This is where Saxon kings battled Norman invaders and Merlin wielded his wand.

Hampton Court
www.the-eye.com/hcgardens.htm
Thirteen miles southwest of London, Hampton Court is one of the finest Tudor palaces and it exudes a royal history.

Cardinal Wolsey, Henry VIII's Lord Chancellor, built the palace five centuries ago with the intention of making it the greatest palace in all the land. He was so successful that Henry became jealous. When Wolsey fell from favor, he offered the palace to Henry in an attempt to get back in his good graces. It didn't work, but Henry took the palace anyway and spent much of the rest of his life in it.

Over the centuries, several regal residents have commissioned new touches to the palace. Architect Christopher Wren was hired to remodel large sections of it and the grounds were inspired by the gardens at Versailles. The shrubbery maze was contributed by Wren. Legend holds that the ghost of Catherine Howard, one of Henry VIII's ill-fated wives, still haunts Hampton Court.

INCREDIBLE NEO-GOTHIC ARCHITECTURE IS OXFORD'S MOST MEMORABLE FEATURE TODAY. THE TOWN'S ORIGINAL NAME IS DERIVED FROM A SHALLOW PART OF THE THAMES WHERE OXEN COULD CROSS OR FORD THE RIVER.

Oxford
www.oxlink.co.uk
www.oxfordcity.co.uk

Described by oft-quoted poet Mathew Arnold as "that sweet city with her dreaming spires," Oxford is home to England's oldest university. A Saxon princess founded the city in the eighth century. Medieval **Carfax Tower** still marks an ancient crossroads. To walk the streets of Oxford is to walk in the footsteps of some of Britain's greatest writers, scientists and politicians. This is the quintessential academic town, full of bookstores, contemplative river walks, and a lively student atmosphere. A short walk in almost any direction will lead you to one of the town's 36 colleges, the earliest of which dates back to the 13th century. **Magdalen College** (**www.magd.ox.ac.uk**), which dominates High Street, was once described as "the most noble and rich structure in the learned world." The most spectacular college, however, might be **Christ Church**, (**www.chch.ox.ac.uk**), which boasts the city's cathedral and a tower designed by Christopher Wren. Christ Church's alumni roster is impressive and includes the likes of King Edward VII and writer Lewis Carroll, author of *Alice in Wonderland*.

Lewis Carroll, whose real name was Charles Dodgson, was a mathematics instructor at Oxford. He captivated the world with his children's fantasy novels, which included **Alice's Adventures in Wonderland** *and* **Through the Looking Glass.** *Carroll based his main character on Alice Liddell, the daughter of the dean of Christ Church.*

Cricket
www-uk.cricket.org

During your visit to England, you're bound to hear talk about one of the country's favorite national pastimes, cricket. To the casual observer, the game seems incomprehensible. Cricket incites great passion in its fans, however. Games usually last a day or more—and even then there's no guarantee of a winner. For a novice, the draw of cricket is the atmosphere. It's all rousing good fellowship, drinks galore and plenty of saucy conversation.

Woodstock
www.oxlink.co.uk/woodstock

Before the Norman conquest, forests stretched across this part of England and royalty kept hunting lodges in Woodstock, a small town about eight miles northwest of Oxford. The early Saxon king Alfred the Great is rumored to have stayed here in the ninth century, and in the 10th century Ethelred the Unready held a council here, suggesting that the size of Woodstock had grown fit to accommodate a king. Geoffrey Chaucer, who penned *The Canterbury Tales*, lived in Woodstock for a time.

Blenheim Palace
www.blenheimpalace.com

Centuries ago, glove-making was Woodstock's chief industry. Today, the town prospers more from visitors who come to see this stately palace. Built for John Churchill, the first Duke of Marlborough, Blenheim Palace was a gift of gratitude from the king for Churchill's victory over the French. Another illustrious ancestor, Sir Winston Churchill, was born at Blenheim Palace in 1874 and is buried nearby.

Today, the 11th Duke of Marlborough lives in old-English style at Blenheim Palace with hundreds of acres of rolling hillsides, a private lake and perfectly manicured gardens. You can catch a miniature train from the palace to the "pleasure garden," where you can play on oversized checkerboards and miniature putting greens and find your way out of yet another garden maze. The butterfly house is superior to most, as it's full of butterflies.

Abingdon
www.oxlink.co.uk/abingdon

This site was settled in ancient times and became a flourishing town during England's Roman period. Abingdon's real glory, however, came in the seventh century when a nephew of the king was granted land for founding a monastery here. Be sure to check out the restored **Checker Hall**, which is used today as an Elizabethan-style theater.

During the Middle Ages, monasteries were the centers of power in the country because Benedictine orders were an important part of the feudal system. So great was the control of Abingdon Abbey that in the 14th century the townspeople—with the help of the mayor and Oxford students—rose up in rebellion against the monks. It wasn't until 200 years later, when Henry VIII dissolved the monasteries, that Abingdon Abbey fell from power.

Vale of White Horse

The Vale of White Horse, which takes its name from the gigantic prehistoric figure of a horse carved into a hillside, is a rich clay valley that stretches south of Abingdon for about 17 miles. No one knows for sure who carved the horse or why they did, though there are many theories. The simplest is that the horse was an ancient road sign.

Wantage
www.oxlink.co.uk/wantage

England's early Saxon king Alfred the Great was born here, and Thomas Hardy sent Jude the Obscure here as an apprentice stonecutter.

Stonehenge

A short drive away lies the most famous and puzzling prehistoric monument in Europe. With its circle of upright ancient stones standing alone on Salisbury Plain, Stonehenge seems to inspire all who visit it. What might be most amazing about this stone circle is that it dates to before 3000 B.C. Moreover, scholars can't seem to figure out why or even how it was built. Some evidence suggests that Stonehenge was used as a place of religious worship or of sacrifice to the moon and the sun, or as a site for festivals.

A henge is defined as an earthen rampart usually enclosing a wood or stone circle. Stonehenge's 50-ton sandstone pieces were carved from rock that is found about 20 miles away—it's still unclear how the stones were moved to this site. Inside the earthen bank are two of four original **Station Stones** *that may have been used for charting the movements of the planets. The* **Heel Stone** *casts a shadow directly into the heart of Stonehenge at midsummer. Each year during the summer solstice, people gather here to watch the sun rise in perfect alignment to the circle. There are some who believe that Stonehenge's builders had a sophisticated knowledge of astronomy. In fact, Stonehenge is located at the only latitude in England at which the extremes of the sun's rising and setting are at right angles to one another.*

Winchester
www.winchester.gov.uk

Sometimes referred to as the "City of Kings," Winchester touts an ancient heritage and impeccably regal credentials. It was in this small English city that monarchs lived, ruled and died and bishops vied for power. In Alfred the Great's time, Winchester was England's Royal City, and William the Conqueror based his government here. Today, portions of William's castle remain, including a mysterious roundtable that supposedly was used by King Arthur and his noble knights.

The historical facts of King Arthur's life have become impossibly mixed with fiction and myth. In the fifth century, there was most likely a leader called Arthur who defended the British against the Saxon invasions. Arthur appears in both pagan and Christian legends. The Christian version focuses on the search for the Holy Grail, the cup from which Jesus drank during the Last Supper and that was believed to have been brought to England. While we'll probably never know the true story of Arthur, the endurance of the myth surrounding him reflects the human love of storytelling and the wistful dreams of an ideal age.

PREHISTORIC STONEHENGE IS MORE THAN 5,000 YEARS OLD.
WHY AND HOW IT WAS BUILT REMAINS A MYSTERY.

Winchester's magnificent cathedral bears witness to this town's former status. From the outside, the cathedral seems unassuming and sedate. Step through its doors, however, and those impressions quickly fade. The 556-foot Gothic nave is the longest in Europe. In the choir, medieval monks sang their eight daily services and celebrated High Mass. Above, a woodland scene shows a knight with his sword at the ready and a falconer with his bird of prey. The crypt houses a well directly under the high altar which some believe predates the church's 11th-century construction. Among the names found inside is one that will be familiar to fans of romantic English fiction—Jane Austen.

After her father's death, Jane Austen, her mother and her sister moved to the town of Chawton. Before she came here, none of Austen's work had been published. The time Austen spent in Chawton was the most prolific and productive of her life. She loved the country and it was here that she found the inspiration to write such classics as Pride & Prejudice, Emma *and* Sense and Sensibility. *Austen, an astute observer of human nature, based her characters and settings on her large circle of friends and their frequent gatherings.* www.hants.gov.uk/austen

SMART DINING

To get the true English experience, you have to visit a pub. "Pubs," short for "Public House," are time-honored English institutions. For centuries, pubs prevailed over churches and marketplaces as preferred social gathering spots. Pubs are a great place

Walking Tours

SMART TIP

If you're up for it, this is some of the best walking country England has to offer. You'll pass old roads where sheep were once herded to market and medieval villages brimming with anecdotes.

to sample basic English "meat-and-two-veg" dishes like steak and kidney pie or chops, potatoes and carrots. To round out the English experience, enjoy a "bitter" with your meal. The beer, a favorite in England, is pumped by hand from the cellar and served at room temperature.

The Bear (Alfred Street), which dates back to 1242, is reputedly Oxford's oldest pub and is usually crowded with students from nearby Christ Church College.

Pubs and Wine Bars in Oxford
www.oxfordcity.co.uk

SMART LODGING

Oxford's streets are lined with honey-colored stone architecture, and you can take your pick of Victorian bed-and-breakfasts or old-style hotels. **The Eastgate Hotel** has the atmosphere of a friendly country house. It's within walking distance of most everything, including the romantic **Magdalen Bridge**.

Rent a Car

SMART TIP

In some parts of England, driving might be your best option, since public transportation isn't available everywhere. A car is also handy for visiting the more remote towns and villages tucked away in the English countryside. Driving here takes a bit of practice, however, as they drive on the left-hand side of the road. Be sure to leave yourself a little extra time to practice.

THE LEGENDS OF ALFRED THE GREAT, KING ARTHUR AND CAMELOT ARE ALIVE AND WELL IN THE ENGLISH COUNTRYSIDE.

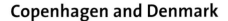

Copenhagen and Denmark

Tourism Web Site: www.visitdenmark.com

A history full of kings and Vikings, home to Hamlet's castle and the birthplace of Hans Christian Andersen. When visiting Denmark, one can't help but think that this is the stuff that legends and fairy tales are made of.

COPENHAGEN
www.aok.dk/Copenhagen

Tourist Office: Vesterbrogade 6 D
1620 Kobenhavn V
Tel: 33111415
Fax: 33931416

Born from the sea, Denmark encompasses 450 islands. Copenhagen itself is located on the island of Sealand. Once a fearsome Viking power that dominated northern Europe, today Denmark is one of the most peaceful and progressive countries in the world, and Copenhagen its largest and liveliest city.

Despite its size, Copenhagen still manages to make travelers feel like they have come upon a small town. Unlike most European capitals, it doesn't have a massive concrete skyline, just a sprinkling of towers and spires. Copenhagen literally means "Merchant's Harbor," but, with its narrow streets, old houses and picturesque canals, it might be better translated to "charm." This is a culture where businessmen bicycle to work, where living well means sharing a simple meal with friends, and where having more isn't necessarily better.

Tivoli
www.tivoligardens.com
The people of Copenhagen know how to live well and they know how to play well. And there's no place they like to play more than at Tivoli, an enchanted amusement park smack-dab in the middle of the city. Like Denmark itself, Tivoli will captivate you.

Since its construction, many rides have been added at Tivoli but the spirit of the park has been the same for 150 years. Tivoli's wooden roller coaster is the world's oldest in operation.

Nyhavn

Nyhavn is the quintessential Copenhagen neighborhood. The canal was carved out 300 years ago so traders could bring wares into the city. Originally home to rowdy sailors, the pastel rows of houses were eventually inhabited by writers, including one by the name of Hans Christian Andersen. The beloved writer of Danish fairy tales lived on the canal at house number 67.

Stroget

Stroget, the longest pedestrian boulevard in Europe, is actually a string of five connecting streets that run from Nyhavn through the city's center. You might consider Stroget Copenhagen's "spine." In Danish, "stroget" means "stroll," but this isn't your basic walk in the park. The energetic mall is crowded with shops and restaurants and people, all of whom seem to be having a good time.

SMART TIP

Canal Boats

Copenhagen has an extensive network of small canals that provide visitors with a peaceful and relaxing way to see the city. Canal tour boats run from the Nytorv end of Nyhavn's harbor from April until mid-September. Check with the local tourist office about daily tours.

If you visit Copenhagen during the summer, you may be rewarded with some impromptu entertainment. For years, Copenhagen has been known for its jazz festival. Drawing musicians from all over the world, the festival takes place at Stroget every July.

Town Hall Square

Town Hall Square is the hub of Copenhagen's commercial district. Here you'll find a statue of Hans Christian Andersen, who wrote such tales as *The Ugly Duckling* and *The Little Mermaid*.

The first "**world clock**" is located in Town Hall. It took inventor Jens Olsen 27 years to complete the timepiece, which calculates actual solar time, or the position of the Earth in relation to the sun. Additionally, the clock has a 570,000-year calendar, shows local time everywhere in the world and boasts a star map that tracks the movement of the Earth's axis.

The Little Mermaid

This life-size bronze statue of Hans Christian Andersen's character, sculpted in 1913, is unquestionably the most popular site in town.

Marmokirken

If you've visited Rome, you may recognize Marmokirken, or "Marble Church." The church's enormous dome was modeled after St. Peter's Cathedral in Vatican City. In the mid-18th century, King Fredrik V ordered construction of this church as part of an ambitious plan to expand the city north. Unfortunately, the project was halted shortly thereafter due to the high cost of Norwegian marble. More than a century later, completion of the church was funded by a wealthy financier.

RUDY SUGGESTS A TOUR BOAT RIDE THROUGH THE CANALS OF COPENHAGEN AS "A GREAT WAY TO DRINK IN THE BEAUTY OF THE CITY AND TO GET YOURSELF ORIENTED FOR MORE SIGHTSEEING."

Royal Library
www.kb.dk

By the mid-20th century, Scandinavian countries were winning praise for innovations in the field of design. The extension to the Royal Library of Copenhagen offers a dazzling example. Its impressive walls slant sharply toward the water, and its façade is covered with reflective black granite tiles imported from Zimbabwe.

Denmark in particular has been a leader in the design of architecture and furniture. At the Dansk Design Center (www.ddc.dk) you can see how Danish designers have set the standard for sleek and uncluttered styles. Their pieces are known around the world for clean lines, graceful shapes and streamlined functionality.

Amalienburg Square

Modern Denmark is a parliamentary democracy. Liberal and progressive, this country enjoys one of the world's highest standards of living. High taxes are balanced by a lower poverty rate and fairer distribution of wealth than in many industrialized nations. Still, tradition reigns. You are visiting the Kingdom of Denmark, where the Queen is much revered and, each day, you can see the changing of the guard at noon in Amalienburg Square.

Dragor

Just a few miles south of Copenhagen, this little town has been preserved just as it was centuries ago. During the Renaissance, Dragor was a high-living fishing port, but today,

---

with its narrow lanes and thatched houses, the town looks like it was lifted from the pages of a storybook.

DRIVING TOUR OF DENMARK

Though Denmark has an excellent public transportation system, if you have the time and the means, renting a car will give you the freedom to explore the countryside at your own pace.

Roskilde
www.vikinger.dk/english/roskilde
About 20 miles west of Copenhagen, on Sealand, is Roskilde, Denmark's first capital and a thriving trade center in the Middle Ages. Roskilde hugs a strategic fjord and in the ninth century A.D. Vikings would set out from here in longboats to raid parts of Europe.

Copenhagen Cards

SMART TIP

If you'll be doing a lot of sightseeing in Copenhagen, drop by the square's tourist office for a Copenhagen Card. The pass gives you unlimited use of trains and buses, as well as access to more than 60 museums and other attractions. You can also pick up a Copenhagen Card at some train stations and hotels. You can catch a bus to Dragor using your Copenhagen Card.

Vikings were the world's best shipbuilders, and with their barbaric attacks they succeeded in terrorizing much of the European coastline. The Vikings' thirst for adventure and profit would eventually drive them as far as Greenland and North America. History, however, has given Vikings a bad rap. While some were raiders, many were peaceful traders and excellent craftsmen.

In 1962, archaeologists excavated a site in Roskilde where they found five well-preserved Viking ships that had been intentionally sunk and piled with rocks. The ships, which included a warship and a trading ship, were reassembled and can be seen at the **Roskilde Viking Ship Museum**.

Lejre Experimental Center
www.lejre-center.dk
If you'd like a taste of how Vikings actually lived, visit the nearby Lejre Experimental Center. Here, where you learn about history by actually doing, you can try your hand at grinding grain or carving wood for boats—using only tools that were available in the past.

North Sealand
Compared to Copenhagen, North Sealand seems very rural and, if possible, more relaxing. Here, rustic woodlands and oceans of fields are spotted with Danish farms. This is the place where locals come to find some quiet and renew their "laid-back" perspective.

Just 20 minutes from Copenhagen, you can join Danes on family outings at **Klampen-borg**. Three hundred years ago, this area was set aside as a royal hunting ground. If you visit, hire a horse for the morning and imagine you're a member of the imperial family

FREDERICKSBORG CASTLE IN HILLEROD WAS THE HOME OF DANISH KINGS
FOR MORE THAN 200 YEARS. OFTEN CALLED THE
"DANISH VERSAILLES," IT'S SCANDINAVIA'S MOST SPECTACULAR CASTLE.

surveying your vast domain. During your ride, you'll be mesmerized by herds of deer that roam the park, including several species that are nearly extinct in other parts of the world.

Hillerod

Enchanted forests encircle this 400-year-old town. At the edge of town, rising like a vision from a lake, you'll find **Fredericksborg Castle**. Sometimes called the "Danish Versailles," this castle is probably the most impressive in all of Scandinavia. At one time, Denmark ruled over practically all of Scandinavia, and for more than 200 years Fredericksborg was home to Danish kings.

Rungstedlund

This is the former home of Karen Blixen, author of *Out of Africa* and other books on aristocratic Danish life. Blixen's father bought this estate in 1879 and Karen was born a few years later. At the age of 28, Blixen entered into a marriage of convenience with her second cousin and moved to Kenya. There, she ran the coffee plantation of which she later wrote so movingly in her novel *Out of Africa*. After the plantation failed and her secret love Denys Finch-Hatton was killed in a plane crash, Blixen returned to Denmark and began her writing career. She lived at Rungstedlund until her death in 1962.

Karen Blixen wrote under the name Isak Dinesen, and it took Danes quite some time to warm to her work, which they perceived as old-fashioned. Eventually, though, her stories became hugely popular in Denmark and around the world. In 1985, a feature film based on Out of Africa *was made starring Meryl Streep and Robert Redford.*

Louisiana Museum of Modern Art
www.louisiana.dk/english
You can use your Copenhagen Card to gain access to this museum, located just a few miles north of Rungstedlund.

The museum offers a collection of works by some of Denmark's most prominent painters and Europe's modern masters. Swiss sculptor Alberto Giacometti's airy figures seem the three-dimensional equivalent of a surrealist painting, and in the idyllic gardens, British artist Henry Moore's subtle, abstract figures stand out like mysterious ancient monoliths.

Helsingor
Hovering on the northeastern tip of Sealand is the shipping town of Helsingor. Centuries ago, the town guarded a sliver of water between Denmark and Sweden. To dominate the water's edge, the Danes built **Kronborg Castle** (**www.kronborgcastle.com**), later immortalized by William Shakespeare as "Elsinore," the setting for *Hamlet*.

At the time Shakespeare was writing Hamlet, *Europe was abuzz with praise for this new fortress. Shakespeare decided it would be the ideal backdrop for the contrasting gloom and splendor of his new play. The characters Rosencrantz and Guildenstern were based on actual Danish nobles visiting the English court during Shakespeare's time. Here fact, fiction and legend intertwine, and prowling the castle that inspired the Bard is great fun.*

SMART DINING

In the late 19th century, Danish bakers went on strike, so Austrian replacements—with their puff pastry techniques—were brought in. When the strike ended, the Danes added their own touches to the puff pastry and the results were sublime. Today, the flaky, mouth-watering pastries are so luscious, they've become known around the world as simply "Danish." It's impossible to visit Denmark without sampling one of its most cherished works of art—the pastry.

Enjoy a meal at **Restaurant Jacobsen**—the famous architect Arne Jacobsen designed the building, and the décor reflects his innovative style. **www.restaurantjacobsen.dk**

SMART LODGING

To find a hotel in Denmark, visit **www.dkhotellist.dk**.

Getting There

SMART TIP

You can travel by train from Copenhagen to Sweden in about 35 minutes. The new bridge that links the two countries was built to promote cultural exchanges and create a single business zone that could compete with other major European hubs.

AFTER TIVOLI GARDENS, ONE OF COPENHAGEN'S MOST POPULAR TOURIST ATTRACTIONS IS THE CHANGING-OF-THE-GUARD CEREMONY AT AMALIENBURG SQUARE.

■ ■ ■ ■   # Amsterdam and The Netherlands

Tourism Web Site: www.holland.com

The Netherlands. This is the country that conquered the sea and a land that inspired such artists as Rembrandt and van Gogh. Citizens of this complex powerhouse of a country know the value of hard work and, perhaps more than in any other country, the value of embracing different cultures.

AMSTERDAM
www.amsterdam.nl

Tourist Office: De Ruyterkade 5
1013 AA Amsterdam
Tel: (+31) (0) 20-551-25-12
E-mail: info@amsterdamtourist.nl

Sometimes called the "Venice of the North," Amsterdam is built around a maze of free-flowing canals. Though the canals were originally built to haul food and wares, today they transport visitors seeking a boats-eye view of the city's gabled architecture.

If you're confused about how you should refer to this area, you're not alone. Holland, Netherlands, Dutch? The country's official title is The Netherlands. Holland technically only refers to the country's two largest counties. For most of us, Holland has become the country's familiar name, and the people who live here are "Dutch."

Dam Square
This is Amsterdam's teeming hub where, eight centuries ago, wanderers from Europe decided to build a dam on the Amstel River, foreshadowing the country's long tradition of wresting land from the sea.

While the rest of Europe struggled to make ends meet in the 17th century, The Netherlands was booming, and Amsterdam was the trading capital of the world. The Dutch fleet contained nearly five times as many ships as the British, and Holland's colonial holdings stretched from Indonesia to the New World. The money poured in and, with it, tulip bulbs from Turkey, porcelain from China and other artifacts that made Amsterdam a truly international city.

Today, as throughout its history, The Netherlands is a huge supporter of the arts. In fact, this country has more art treasures per square mile than any other country in the world.

Rijksmuseum
www.rijksmuseum.nl

The Rijksmuseum, at Stadhouderskade 42, houses an incomparable collection of paintings by the many artists who worked in and around Amsterdam. During the Golden Age, it was fashionable for wealthy city-dwellers to commission local artists. As you'll see from the art here, landscapes and portraits were especially popular.

In Johannes Vermeer's *The Kitchen Maid*, you'll see the artist's fascination with light. In serene interiors, single figures engage in everyday tasks while clear light filters in, evoking a fresh, almost jewel-like glow. Frans Hals, meanwhile, was a master at capturing spontaneity. His *Jolly Toper*, with raised hand, teetering wineglass and twinkling eyes, is a moment of life frozen on canvas. Rembrandt, also featured at the Rijksmuseum, was truly a giant in the history of art. His works, characterized by luxuriant brush strokes and a mastery of light and dark, conveyed a deep understanding of human character. The brilliant *Night Watch* was commissioned as an official portrait of a military company. In the painting, Rembrandt's subjects break from a traditional static pose as they shoulder their weapons, creating a striking image of movement and life.

Jordaan Neighborhood

Its seafaring past and the constant traffic through its port gave Amsterdam a reputation as a tolerant, easygoing town and this neighborhood offers a perfect example. In the 17th century, Jordaan was a refuge for Jews fleeing persecution across Europe. Protestants driven from Catholic France also found this neighborhood to be a safe haven.

NETHERLANDS' NATIVE SON, REMBRANDT, IS A FEATURED ARTIST AT THE RIJKSMUSEUM IN AMSTERDAM.

Anne Frank House
www.channels.nl/amsterdam/annefran.html

On the edge of the Jordaan neighborhood, in the attic of this merchant's house, Anne Frank's family hid from the Nazis from July 1942 until August 1944. In her famous diary, which has since been translated into 60 different languages, Anne Frank describes her family's survival as Jewish persecution in Amsterdam began in earnest. Especially poignant are the pictures of movie stars and celebrities that Anne lovingly pasted to the walls of her dark bedroom. In August 1944, someone betrayed the Franks to the Nazis and they were arrested and sent to concentration camps. Anne Frank died in Bergen-Belsen at the age of 15.

> **SMART TIP**
>
> # Beating the Lines
>
> The Anne Frank House is one of Amsterdam's most popular tourist destinations. Arrive early in the morning or late in the day to avoid long lines.

Westerkerk

In her diary, Frank described the bells of nearby Westerkerk. The Anne Frank house sits in the shadow of the church on the edge of the Jordaan neighborhood. The lofty clock tower, topped by a colorful crown, is the tallest in Amsterdam. The tower was built in tribute to the Hapsburg ruler Maximilian I. According to legend, Maximilian granted the church the privilege to wear his crown because he was miraculously cured of an illness while visiting Amsterdam.

Van Gogh Museum
www.vangoghmuseum.nl

This museum contains the world's largest collection of Vincent van Gogh's art. After the artist took his own life in 1890, his brother Theo, an art dealer, collected 200 of his paintings, 500 hundred of his drawings and hundreds of his letters. They were eventually brought to this museum.

Vincent van Gogh, considered the first great Dutch master of the 19th century, started painting in 1880 and died just a decade later. He spent five years of his tumultuous career in The Netherlands before moving to France. Van Gogh was deeply dissatisfied with the values of industrial society, and an intense sympathy for the poor dominates his early paintings. While other artists of the day pushed impressionism toward a severe, classical style, van Gogh did the opposite, seeking greater freedom to express his emotions. As you'll see in his later works, van Gogh discovered the power of color, using every brush stroke as an expressive graphic gesture.

Red Light District

Amsterdam's liberal, live-and-let-live attitude is probably best represented in the renowned Red Light District. Since the 13th century, prostitution has been a going concern in Amsterdam, but this historic neighborhood holds more than just houses of ill repute.

Amstelkring
www.museumamstelkring.nl

Once the home of a wealthy Dutch merchant, today this little-known museum conceals a fascinating record of life from centuries past. The museum's greatest treasure is the small church built into the top three floors of the house. In the late 16th century, the Dutch government forced the city's large Catholic churches to turn Protestant, though Catholics were allowed to attend services if they were held in private homes such as this. Centuries ago, there were more than 30 hidden churches like this in Amsterdam. Now, Amstelkring is the city's lone survivor.

> *A poet once wrote that Holland is a place "...where the broad ocean leans against the land." And for good reason. Nearly half of Holland is below sea level. With windmills, farmers were able to drain the water from the land, creating fertile soil. As the ocean tried to reclaim the land, however, Holland's legendary battle against flooding began.*

Windmills

Whether you've visited Holland or not, talk of the country invariably conjures images of windmills, and for good reason. Nearly a thousand of the revolving mechanisms gild the Dutch countryside. As early as the 12th century, windmills became the chief source of power in this part of Europe. Windmills enabled farmers to harness wind power for crushing seeds and grinding grain. Their most vital function, however, was to drain the land of water.

FOR MANY TRAVELERS, WINDMILLS ARE THE ENDURING SYMBOL OF HOLLAND. THE PRISTINE COUNTRYSIDE IS STILL DOTTED WITH HUNDREDS OF WORKING WINDMILLS.

MUIDERSLOT CASTLE IS A MUSEUM TODAY. BUT IN THE 13TH CENTURY
IT WAS HOME TO COUNT FLORIS V.

Zaanse Schans
http://zaanseschans.nl

More than two centuries ago, this area, just 15 minutes outside Amsterdam, was one of the world's first industrial parks. Today, Zaanse Schans is still a working village that preserves traditional Dutch industries and crafts. You can visit Zaanse Schans by train. It's about a five-minute walk from the "Koog Zaandijk" station. If you've rented a car you can drive, but you'll probably have to pay for parking.

Muiderslot
www.muiderslot.demon.nl

A few miles southeast of Amsterdam, this fairy-tale castle rises from a moat. Floris V, the Count of Holland, built Muiderslot in the late 13th century.

Floris V helped Amsterdam's finances by allowing citizens of the city to transport their goods along the canals of Holland free of charge. This angered a group of noblemen who thought the Count's generous ways cut into their profits. In 1296, the nobles imprisoned the Count in his own castle and then murdered him.

Heading through south Holland's countryside, you'll feel as though you've been transported into a Dutch master's paintings. But these bucolic scenes belie the region's turbulent history. Sitting on the delta of major European rivers, this area was strategically positioned to dominate trade. Along with Belgium and Luxembourg, Holland was a prize highly contested by the rest of medieval Europe.

The Hague

For three centuries, Holland was controlled by the mighty Hapsburg dynasty. In the 16th century, the harsh rule of the Spanish Hapsburgs led to a revolt by which the northern provinces gained independence. Those provinces ultimately became today's

Netherlands, and the country's major political center developed in The Hague. To get to The Hague from Amsterdam, you'll have to change trains. You can access schedules in Central Station. You can also fly directly to The Hague from the United States.

The Hague is a progressive, international city with a royal pedigree. It was built up around a 13th-century palace built by William, a Count of Holland. Today it's the seat of the Dutch government and home of the International Court of Justice for the United Nations. Like the rest of the country, The Hague seems open to new ideas and different points of view.

Mesdag
www.mesdag.nl

Panorama Mesdag, at Zeestraat 65 in The Hague (tramway 7 or 8 or bus 4, 5, 13 or 22), is the world's largest circular painting. The scene, which depicts a small Dutch fishing village from the late 19th century, spans a circumference of 395 feet. The viewer's platform is a dune, which creates the amazing illusion of actually looking at the sea and Holland's wide beaches. Gazing on the circular canvas, the work of Dutch painter Hendrik Mesdag and his assistants, is like taking a trip through time and space.

SMART TIP

Rent a Bike

In this city, crisscrossed by narrow streets and canal bridges, there's no more suitable form of transportation than the bicycle. Holland is very flat, and the city's transportation system is conveniently biased in favor of bikes. If cycling isn't your thing, buy a "strip ticket," which you can use to board an electric tram. When you board, have the attendant punch your ticket or use one of the machines located in the rear of the tram. Always cancel one strip more than the number of zones you're traveling.

FROM RUDY MAXA'S TRAVELER NEWSLETTER

The Four Successful Keys to Family Travel
How to stay sane on a road trip with kids—from a dad who knows!

If you've been a parent as long as I have (24 years of service so far), you probably know the joy of traveling with your children. But my guess is that you've also survived some hellish trips. And why not? After all, no school teaches parents how to travel smart with kids. But there are ways to enjoy the experience. Here are my best tips for arranging a great kid-parent trip.

1. Agree on the agenda.

You'd be surprised at the number of families who plan trips without consulting everyone traveling. Over dinner, or at a special family meeting, make it clear what an upcoming trip is about. Is mom or dad traveling on business and desirous of bringing along a child? Or are you making plans for a kids' vacation?

If it's the former, your child or children will understand from the outset that you'll have to do some work while on the road. If it's a pure kids' vacation, then almost everything ought to be about the kids.

There are all kinds of reasons to travel with children besides to see relatives. How about turning a trip to check out a college for a high school junior into a vacation for the rest of the family? Why not spice up a school assignment by doing some on-site research?

Most importantly, keep the kids involved. Let them go online and do some research about your destination. Or maybe they can find reading for the rest of the family that will make the experience richer. Encourage a child to learn how to read a map by putting him or her in charge of plotting out your route—even if you're flying.

2. Be prepared.

Keep a notepad handy in the days leading up to travel. Write down anything you happen to think of that you need to bring along, from a young child's favorite toy or blanket to electronic games or a Walkman for teenagers.

Want a special kids' meal on a flight? Remember, you must order that at least 24 hours before departure. Need reservations at a ball game or cultural event at your destination? Call ahead for tickets. If you're staying at a hotel with a concierge, don't be shy about calling long before you travel, asking what events will be going on when you're there and, if necessary, arranging for tickets.

Call your airline the morning of your departure to make sure your flight is on time; waiting hours for a delayed takeoff in an airport with young children can be difficult for all involved.

Be sure to ask what kind of beds you have in your hotel or motel room ahead of time. A "double room" might only mean a double bed. If you need more beds, make sure you reserve them early.

3. Budget, but don't sweat it.

If you're trying to teach your children about the value of money, let them know how you ordered airline tickets ahead of time to save. Or explain why driving is sometimes cheaper for a family than taking a train or plane. Allocate a certain amount of money for each child to spend each day to help prevent the familiar refrain, "Mommy, will you buy me that?" Remember, you'll always spend more than you expect. So build a cushion so you stay cool when you get a bit off budget.

4. Don't overdo it—and celebrate your memories.

The most common mistake I think families make on vacations is trying to do too much. Always build in down time, especially when young children are involved. Try not to drive more than a few hours a day. Remember, you can't see everything on every trip. Listen to your kids—if they're getting tired and cranky, call it a day. Hang by the hotel pool or take a quiet walk along the beach.

Don't treat meals as necessary interruptions. Try to find a local restaurant. A child can find regional accents, local foods and dishes, and even architecture exotic and (dare I say it?) educational. And meals are ideal times to interact with local residents.

Or designate dinner out as a special time to review the day's adventures, and pack a picnic for lunch. The advantages are two-fold: First, picnicking in a scenic spot along your route doesn't take away as much time from sightseeing or getting where you're headed. Second, it's much easier on smaller children than holding them captive in a restaurant seat for an hour or more.

Remember, too, that photos really do capture memories. Make a scrapbook when you return. Write a funny story or two. Keep a couple of special menus or a program from a sporting or cultural event. Trust me. Creating a family archive will be meaningful to both you and your children in the future.

P.S. HEADS UP!

Traveling abroad as a single parent with your child? Some countries, such as Mexico, require that if you're traveling with a minor, you carry a recently notarized letter of permission from the other parent. No letter? No admission. The goal is to thwart kidnapping by noncustodial parents. So check with the embassy or consulate of the country you intend to visit to check out local regulations.

Madurodam
www.madurodam.nl

The diminutive city of Madurodam, one of the highlights of The Hague, offers a completely different look at the Dutch countryside. This is an entire town in miniature, a 1-to-25-scale reproduction of a fictitious Dutch city. In its tiny living landscape, trains run, ships sail and there's an ongoing town fair. Visitors to Madurodam tromp up and down its little streets like Gulliver in the land of Lilliput. Whether you're traveling with a real kid, or just the kid within, Madurodam is a delight.

Delft

Ten miles southeast of The Hague, Delft has canals, bridges and stretches of gabled facades that feel like a scene from a Vermeer painting.

Delft has become nearly synonymous with the distinctive blue and white china that is produced here. True to Holland's international heritage, it was Italian immigrants who first introduced glazed pottery here. When the Dutch East Indies Company brought porcelain back from China, however, local potters quickly adopted the Chinese method of creating fine blue and white vases and plates.

SMART DINING

Whether you're sampling herring at a street stand or dining in a fine restaurant, good food isn't hard to find in Holland. Amsterdam, with its melting-pot character, has adopted culinary influences from around the world and the Dutch have very high standards.

As a result of Holland's former colonial dominance in the East Indies, the Dutch have enthusiastically adopted Indonesian food. Rijsttafel, or "rice table," is a banquet of rice or noodles with countless spicy side dishes.

Restaurant **Puri Mas** (**www.purimas.nl**), located in Amsterdam's Leidseplein neighborhood, serves some of the tastiest rijsttafel in town.

Rent a Car

SMART TIP

Some of Holland's most engaging historical sights are located just outside Amsterdam. To explore areas outside the city, you can use Holland's excellent public transportation system or rent a car. For information on renting a car overseas, check the Avis web site at **www.avis.com**.

▨ ▨ ▨ ■ Belgium

Tourism Web Site: www.belgium-tourism.com

They say good things come in small packages, and Belgium is no exception. Just about the size of Maryland, Belgium is a tapestry of culture, history and language divided into two areas: Dutch-speaking Flanders in the north, and French-speaking Wallonia in the south. For nearly two centuries, these two groups have managed to balance their patriotic spirit with their historic differences.

Tucked between northern and southern Europe, Belgium was historically an attractive pawn for its more powerful neighbors. The bigwigs of Europe passed this small country back and forth for nearly a thousand years. For a time, the Dukes of Burgundy claimed it, then it was the Hapsburgs, and Napoleon met his Waterloo not far from Brussels. When the French handed Belgium to the Dutch about 200 years ago, the people here decided they'd had enough and rebelled against the outsiders.

Following the Belgian revolution in the early 19th century, Belgians fiercely guarded their personal liberties, which included free speech and freedom of the press. As a result, Brussels became a refuge for writers and intellectuals and even home to such luminaries as Victor Hugo and Karl Marx.

If this is your first visit, here's a quick tip about Belgians—they love the arts, they celebrate great beer, they savor superb chocolate and, as a rule, they appreciate the good things in life and are willing to work hard to get them.

BRUSSELS
www.expatriate-online.com

Tourist Office: BITC BRUSSEL
Stadhuis
Grote Markt
1000 Brussels
Tel: 02/513-89-40
Fax: 02/513-83-20
www.tourism.brussels@tib.be

RUDY BOARDS A CARRIAGE TO ENJOY THE GOTHIC PLEASURES OF THE GRAND PLACE, BRUSSELS' CENTRAL SQUARE. IN THE BACKGROUND IS CITY HALL. AMAZINGLY, THE GRAND PLACE ESCAPED MAJOR DAMAGE FROM THE HEAVY BOMBING OF BRUSSELS DURING WORLD WAR II.

Brussels, home of the European Union and headquarters of NATO, is Europe's unofficial capital. As a result, among the city's generous verdant spaces and inventive architecture, you'll find more ambassadors than in any other spot in the world.

Grand Place

The Grand Place, Brussels' splendid central square, has always been the heart of the city. In medieval times, when merchant guilds dominated the economic life of Brussels, trade associations showed off their considerable wealth with fancy headquarters, or "guild houses." The Grand Place is encircled by such houses.

Brussels' **Town Hall** dates back to the early 1400s, when the city was booming thanks to the cloth trade. Today, this is where you'll find Brussels' excellent tourist office.

Manneken Pis

The locals regard this statue of a mischievous lad, located about a block away from the Grand Place, as a symbol of their irreverent spirit. While there are many legends as to how the young boy became immortalized, the most famous claims he put out the burning fuse of a bomb that threatened the Grand Place by using the most natural of extinguishing methods (ahem). He may or may not be your cup o' tea, but Manneken Pis has earned quite a following from fans around the world. Many of them show their admiration by sending costumes to add to his wardrobe. City officials regularly dress him in different selections. Items from Manneken Pis's unique closet are displayed in the Museum of the City of Brussels.

Theatre Royal de Toone

Centuries ago, puppet shows hooked audiences in much the same way soap operas do today. In Belgium, there were hundreds of puppet theaters scattered across the countryside. Many puppet theaters were bombed out during WWII, but this one, Theater

Toone, survived and is run today by the seventh generation of a puppeteering dynasty. With more than a thousand puppets in its collections, Theater Toone is always ready to take a stab at an old classic.

Royal Museum of Fine Arts
www.fine-arts-museum.be

Nobles may have built the castles in Belgium, but it was the country's backbone, its staunch middle class, that forged the cities and commissioned works of art. As a result, there are more than 70 museums in Brussels alone. At the Royal Museum of Fine Arts, you can view the originals of masters including Peter Paul Rubens, Salvador Dali, Pieter Bruegel the Elder and Jacques-Louis David. Many believe Pieter Bruegel the Elder was the single greatest genre painter of the 16th century. He was a genius at combining biblical and moral allusions with scenes from everyday peasant life. In *The Fall of Icarus*, the mythological hero disappears into the sea while the village people continue about their daily business.

Jacques-Louis David, who took an active part in the French revolution, spent years of exile in Belgium after Napoleon's empire collapsed. In Death of Marat, he depicts the revolutionary leader after he's been murdered in his bathtub. David's neoclassic style and his deep feelings for the issues of the day allowed him to create this astonishingly stark and moving portrait.

Musical Instruments Museum
www.mim.fgov.be

Belgium's reputation as a refuge from repressive regimes fostered a thriving art scene well into the 19th and 20th centuries that touched not only its paintings but its architecture as well.

One of Brussels' most famous art nouveau–style buildings currently houses the city's Musical Instruments Museum. In fantastically designed displays, the collection embraces instruments from around the world throughout the ages. Thankfully, the museum's planners believed that musical instruments should be seen *and* heard, so, using headphones and infrared technology, visitors can listen to about 200 musical extracts.

The Musical Instruments Museum puts a special emphasis on Belgian musical traditions, which include the dulcimer, the drum and bagpipes. The dulcimer, which originated in the Middle East, was brought to Belgium by the religious crusaders of the 12th century. The instrument was especially popular with women and girls. Drums, the heartbeat of Belgian processions for centuries, were popular among the military and the archers' guild. Bagpipes were the favorite instrument of shepherds, who relied on music to keep their animals calm and to prevent them from straying.

Cathedral

Brussels' magnificent cathedral is located between lower and upper town on Treurenberg Hill. Its Gothic choir was begun in 1226 and completed three centuries later. Hapsburg emperor Charles V and the 16th-century governors, who seem to have had a special fondness for this Gothic masterpiece, bestowed the stained glass windows. Though Protestant reformers ransacked the church's early work, over the centuries much of the decoration has been restored. Be sure to check out the wooden pulpit carved by an Antwerp sculptor around the turn of the 18th century. In the carving, angels are depicted driving Adam and Eve from paradise toward skeletons of death.

Atomium
www.atomium.be

Brussels' most original monument by far is the Atomium, a cluster of giant spheres that represent the atomic structure of an iron molecule enlarged 165 billion times. The Atomium, built for the 1958 World's Fair, is a celebration of the spirit of science.

Atomium

SMART TIP

For a spectacular view of the city, take an elevator to the top of the Atomium.

Belgian Comic Strip Center

Leave it to the Belgians to create the world's first museum dedicated to the art of the comic strip. Located in an art nouveau building at Zandstraat, Rue des Sables, 20 – 000 Brussels, the exhibits here trace comic strips from their earliest forms to their most recent incarnations.

First appearing in the 1920s, Belgium's most beloved character, Tintin, has become popular throughout the world. The adventures of the young reporter and his smart-aleck dog have sold more than 200 million books by Herge. Always on the side of good, globetrotting Tintin and four-legged Snowy get themselves in the most amazing predicaments. But just when it seems that all is lost, Tintin manages to find his way out of trouble.

PUPPET THEATRES ARE A BELGIUM TRADITION THAT STILL THRIVES TODAY. HERE, BONACIEU AND D'ARTAGNAN OF THREE MUSKETEERS FAME PRACTICE DUELING WITH THEIR SWORDS. THE PUPPETS ARE THE CREATION OF THEATRE TOONE IN BRUSSELS.

Lower Town

Just off the Grand Place, lower town is a patchwork of quirky streets and squares. During a walk through this neighborhood, you'll see musicians playing, street vendors hawking their wares and artists plying their trades.

Upper Town

This is where stylish locals come to escape the city hubbub and make the scene. As early as the 18th century, Brussels' political center had begun to shift to upper town. Spurred by the ambitions of early kings, this is where the modernization of Belgium quickly became evident.

Royal Museum for Central Africa
www.africamuseum.be

Located just outside the city in the suburb of Tervuren, this museum was founded to celebrate Belgium's colonial empire in the Belgian Congo (now the Democratic Republic of Congo). Though the museum was once considered an imperialist showpiece, it has been updated to focus on African tribal culture and wildlife.

After ascending to the throne in 1865, Leopold II wanted to expand his empire. Aided by explorer Henry Stanley, Leopold grabbed control of a huge portion of Central Africa for himself, with no parliament to curb his power. Over the next several decades he became enormously wealthy through slave trade and the exploitation of African people and land. An international outcry against atrocities committed under Leopold's rule eventually forced the Belgian parliament to strip him of his fiefdom and annex the colony to the nation.

BRUGES
www.bruges.be

Tourist Office:	Toerisme BRUGGE
	Burg 11
	8000 Brugge
	Tel: 050/44-86-86
	Fax: 050/44-86-00
	E-mail: toerisme@brugge.be

Bruges, once considered the capital of medieval northern Europe, is about an hour's drive northwest of Brussels.

Until the 16th century, Bruges was one of the most successful and wealthy cities in Europe. After its lucrative textile industry developed, merchants came here from all over Europe to buy and sell silk, fish and furs. So successful was the trade in Bruges that Europe's first stock exchange was established here. But when the town's river dried up and competition from English weavers grew, Bruges fell on hard times, and much of the town's trade shifted to Antwerp.

Like a sleeping beauty, Bruges existed practically undisturbed for 400 years. Today, like an open-air museum, it appears a perfectly preserved medieval fairy town, complete with guild houses, castles and spires. Walking around Bruges, you'll spy graceful swans gliding across glassy canals, cobbled streets and quiet corners where time seems to have stood still.

Markt

This is a great place to start a walking tour of Bruges. The large open square pulses with pedestrians and horse-drawn carriages, and everywhere you look you'll find a medieval guild house. Of course, most of them have been converted to restaurants, including one where, in the 15th century, town leaders imprisoned Archduke Maximilian of Austria for three weeks because he attempted to restrict their privileges. When he later became the Holy Roman Emperor, he repaid his former captors by redirecting trade to Antwerp.

Gruuthuse Museum

This museum, at Dijver 17 – 8000 Brugge, gives visitors a feel for how the well-off lived in medieval times. The honorary Lords of Gruuthuse were powerful figures in Bruges because they held a monopoly on *gruut*, a mixture of herbs and flowers used to flavor beer. At the time, beer was the most popular drink around because it was boiled during processing, making it safer to drink than water.

During Bruges' heyday, the town's citizens earned a reputation for their snazzy dressing. Throughout Europe, the well-to-do were decking themselves out in lacy finery and Bruges soon became lace-making central. During the Middle Ages, a thriving cottage industry produced lace for the European market. At the time, women of every social class adopted the skill and for centuries wound thread into increasingly intricate patterns.

Beguinage

The religious crusades of the Middle Ages created a shortage of men. Many women, instead of relying on the charity of family members, chose to enter organized communities, or Beguinages. The women who joined these communities were not nuns, but they took vows of chastity and led simple, modest lives praying, making lace and caring for the sick and the poor. If a woman in a Beguinage found a husband, she was free to leave. Today, Benedictine nuns clothed in 15th century–style vestments occupy the Beguinage's tranquil houses.

Cathedral of Our Lady

The cathedral, one of Bruges' greatest treasures, took 200 years to complete and houses Michelangelo's marble sculpture *Madonna and Child*. When his original client failed to pay for the statue, the artist sold it to a merchant from Bruges—it was the only one of Michelangelo's works to leave Italy in his lifetime. Beyond the famous sculpture, the church is a treasury of art and pious decoration.

THE MEDIEVAL CANALED CITY OF BRUGES IS OFTEN CALLED THE "VENICE OF THE NORTH." A TOUR-BOAT RIDE IS A HIGHLIGHT OF ANY VISIT TO BRUGES, JUST 45 MINUTES WEST OF BRUSSELS BY TRAIN.

SMART DINING

When I think of fine cuisine, Belgium is hardly the first country that comes to mind. The truth is, Belgians are passionate about their food, and Brussels has more gourmet restaurants per capita than Paris. **Le Falstaff** restaurant, Rue Henri Maus 17–23, is a great place to sample Belgian specialties. Inside the restaurant, impressive stained glass windows narrate Shakespeare's *Falstaff* legend. The national obsession in Belgium is mussels and fries and the chefs here have elevated this basic fare to an art form. For the true Belgian experience, top off your traditional meal with a beer—Le Falstaff offers more than 300 brews.

SMART LODGING

Just a block off the Grand Place is **Hotel Amigo**, which may very well have the most convenient location in town. In old Belgian slang, "amigo" meant prison and, in fact, there was once a prison on this very site. Today, the plush hotel is about as far from prison as you can get. Hotel Amigo's claim to fame is its understated luxury and its location. **www.hotelamigo.com**

Paris

Tourism Web Site: www.paris-tourism.com

Tourist Office: 127, avenue des Champs-Elysées – 75008 Paris
RER: Charles-de-Gaulle-Etoile
Metro: George V
Tel: 33 (0) 8-36-68-31-12 (2,21 FFR/min)
Fax: 33 (0) 1-49-52-53-00
www.paris-touristoffice.com
E-mail: info@paris-touristoffice.com

> **RUDY:**
> Chunnel Information (Paris, London, Brussels): The Chunnel is a fast track
> to savings. Tickets for the 31-mile Channel Tunnel between London and
> Paris or Brussels have cost as much as $120 one-way Standard Class, compared
> with around $20 for the old-fashioned ferry. But experiencing a miracle of
> mechanical technology just got more affordable: You can now buy a round-
> trip ticket on the Eurostar instead of two standard one-way tickets. Visit
> **www.raileurope.com** or call 800-EUROSTAR. For basic information about
> Eurostar, go to **www.eurostar.com**.

Paris—the City of Light, home of the impressionists, existentialists, haute couture and haute cuisine. In this city, life is art.

Since the Middle Ages, scholars, philosophers and artists have flocked to Paris, and with them came new ideas and a spirit of inquiry and change. If you're serious about getting to know Paris, stroll down the city's grand boulevards and parks and indulge in its exceptional food and wine.

Parisians seem to be born with style, and everything they do, from displaying pastries to designing department stores, they do with flair.

The city is split in half by the River Seine. The Right Bank, where you'll find the Louvre, the Tuileries, the Champs Elysees and an abundance of high fashion, is the upscale side of town. The Left Bank, where you'll find the Sorbonne, the Musée d'Orsay and the Eiffel Tower, is known for its bohemian, student atmosphere.

THE CHURCHES OF PARIS OFFER GLIMPSES OF THE CITY'S RICH HISTORY AND A TREASURY OF ART. NOTRE DAME CATHEDRAL IS ONE OF THE BEST KNOWN, BUT RUDY URGES TRAVELERS TO CHECK OUT SEVERAL OTHERS, TOO.

Notre Dame
www.paris.org/Monuments/NDame

The Parisian desire to reach for the sky started early. Notre Dame de Paris was begun in 1100, springing out of a new, popular idea—the celebration of the Virgin Mother. Before the 11th century, the Virgin had played only a minor role in Christian religion. After the crusades and contact with the East, however, focus shifted from heavy, masculine structures to light, feminine structures dedicated to the Virgin.

Cathedrals like Notre Dame, with their stunning stained-glass windows, sprang up all over France. For the common people who spent most of their lives in small dark dwellings, these airy Gothic cathedrals, lighted by windows, were marvelous.

Climb the 300 steps to the top of Notre Dame to work off those pastries, take in an excellent view of the city and cozy up to the gargoyles for which the church is famous. The original medieval gargoyles gradually wore away and from time to time toppled over the side, landing with a crash on the pavement below. In the 19th century, new gargoyles took their place as the guardians of Notre Dame.

The Latin Quarter

Cross the Petit Pont near Notre Dame to get to the Latin Quarter, named for the language scholars spoke here. The University of Paris, the Sorbonne, drew scholars from all over the

SMART TIP

Books

Take a walk along the Seine while you're in the Latin Quarter. You might be surprised to find that the stands aren't selling hot dogs and beer, but—true to the area's tradition of education—books, books, and more books.

world. In the 13th century, the streets of this section of town were like open-air classrooms. Seated on straw, students would take in lectures from such instructors as the famed Italian poet Dante.

Today, learning and experimenting continues in the Latin Quarter. Students fill the streets, and the area is a lively mixture of bookstores, cinemas and fast food.

St. Severin in the Latin Quarter is worth a look for its stained glass—old and new—alone, but also of note are the twisted columns and flamboyant Gothic architecture.

Pompidou Center (Metro station Rambuteau)
www.cnac-gp.fr

When architects Richard Rogers and Renzo Piano completed the Centre Pompidou in 1977, Parisians were outraged. They complained that the building showed a lack of respect for the historic character and architecture of the city. Depending on your taste, you may agree. The Pompidou is a building turned inside out. Electrical tubes, water pipes and ventilation ducts, each color-coded by function, run outside the structure. After its completion, the Pompidou Center became very popular, and it currently outdistances the Louvre and the Eiffel Tower in number of visitors.

At the top of the Pompidou Center, you'll find a modern art museum that houses an exceptional collection of work from the 20th century.

You'll find the playful **Stravinsky Fountain** next door to the Pompidou Center. The fountain was installed in 1983 and inspired by the compositions of composer Igor Stravinsky.

THESE WHIMSICAL SCULPTURES ARE A PART OF THE STRAVINSKY FOUNTAIN NEXT TO THE POMPIDOU CENTER. THE FOUNTAIN IS A SUPERB EXAMPLE OF PARIS'S LOVE AFFAIR WITH ART IN PUBLIC PLACES.

TODAY, THE ENDURING SYMBOL OF PARIS IS THE EIFFEL TOWER. BUT THAT WASN'T ALWAYS THE CASE. WHEN IT WAS BUILT IN 1889 MANY LOCALS OBJECTED VOCALLY TO THE "UGLY MONSTROSITY."

Eiffel Tower

Sometimes it seems that each new addition to the streets of Paris generates controversy, but that never stops the drive to innovate. Even the Eiffel Tower, once described as a useless monstrosity, was ridiculed.

Gustave Eiffel built the Tower for the World's Fair of 1889 with the intention of tearing it down once the Fair was over. Those plans were scrapped when Parisians realized the tower had become the symbol of their city.

Paris Markets

If you'd like more detailed information about roving Parisian markets, pick up *Paris in a Basket* by Meyer and Smith. The streets of Paris are crowded with markets, large and small. Some markets operate daily, like the flower market on the **Ile de la Cité**, but others are spontaneous affairs that spring up on the weekends. On Sundays, I always keep my eye out for antique markets.

Luxembourg Palace and the Tuileries

Each of these sites was built to indulge homesick members of the Medici family. Marie de Medici, widow of Henry IV, had the Luxembourg Palace and gardens built to remind her of the Pitti Palace in her native city of Florence, while Catherine de Medici,

> **SMART TIP**
>
> Parisian parks, with their manicured trees and immaculate lawns, offer pleasant strolling or a place for a picnic lunch, but keep in mind that in most Parisian parks, it is forbidden to walk or sit on the grass.

the Queen, had had the Tuileries built 50 years earlier to remind her of an Italian park. With the Louvre as the backdrop, the Tuileries still have a regal air.

The Louvre
www.louvre.fr

The Louvre is possibly the best-known museum in the world. To avoid seeing the *Mona Lisa* over the heads of a small army, take advantage of evening hours and try to avoid weekends!

Musée d'Orsay
www.musee-orsay.fr

Apart from the Louvre, this is Paris' other preeminent museum. Formerly a train station, this grand museum houses art from the 1840s to the first World War, but it is best known for its collection of impressionist works. The Orsay includes works by Renoir, Monet and van Gogh.

At the first impressionist exhibit in 1874, critics and the public alike condemned the new style, calling it childish and amateur. One critic described the impressionist works as "less finished than the crudest wallpaper." The impressionists rejected the classical realism of paintings of the time, presenting the world as they perceived it in a moment. Impressionist paintings were shocking because they were infused with all the emotions and sensations their creators felt in an instant.

Montmartre

In the 19th century, impressionists, and later cubists, gathered in this rural area located on the Right Bank, up north in the 18th arrondissement. The church Sacre-Coeur, which offended many Parisians when it was built in 1914, dominates Montmartre.

Today, Montmartre's central square is the lively **Place de Tertre**, where street artists earn a living as they entertain passersby. But in the back streets you can still find traces of the rural Montmartre the impressionists knew. Artists including Renoir and Picasso frequented **The Lapin Agile** cabaret, which is still open in the evenings for shows.

Rodin Museum (Metro stop: Varenne)
www.musee-rodin.fr

The Rodin museum isn't far from **Les Invalides**, and its garden provides a lovely setting for art.

Sculptor Auguste Rodin, a master at capturing the drama of a single moment, was a contemporary of the impressionists, and critics

Avoid Crowds

SMART TIP

To avoid crowds, visit the museum on Sunday mornings or when it's open late on Thursday evenings.

You can buy a one-, three- or five-day multi-museum pass at major Metro stops or museums. Not only will this option save you money, the pass allows you to bypass the lines to get in.

Time-Saver

If you're short on time, the gardens at the museum have their share of great works and can be seen in a brief visit.

SHOPPING FOR PICNIC SUPPLIES ALONG THE RUE CLER NEAR THE EIFFEL TOWER IS A QUICK AND EASY IMMERSION INTO FRENCH CULTURE AND MANNERS. FOR RUDY AND MANY TRAVELERS, BRIDGING THE LANGUAGE BARRIER IS HALF THE FUN.

misunderstood him as well. Most famous of all his works is *Le Penseur—The Thinker—* a man weighed down by his own thoughts. In his portrait of Balzac, Rodin masterfully captures the French writer in a moment of determined concentration. In *The Burghers of Calais*, he depicts the reaction of six men who are forced to abandon their town to an invading army.

Paris Shopping

If you haven't noticed it yet, Parisians have a certain "je ne sais quoi." If you're after that hip Parisian look, there are several streets near the **Place Vendôme** (**www.place-vendome.net**) and the famous **Ritz Hotel** (**www.ritzparis.com**) with top-of-the-line designer houses.

If you can't afford these particular shops, don't despair. The department stores in Paris are top of the line. Make a stop at **Galeries Lafayette** for anything from trendy designer clothing to French perfume.

Marais

Marais is a former swamp located on the right bank of the Seine.

In 1612, the neighborhood was perked up by the **Place des Vosges**, a royal residence that housed princesses, duchesses and writers like Victor Hugo and Molière. In the 17th century, nobles engaged in midnight duels at the Place.

Tax Refund

SMART TIP

If you spend over a certain amount in one store, you can get the hefty value-added tax returned to you. Ask for the details before you buy. At the airport, when you leave the European community, find the customs office and apply for your refund.

Many of the grand hotels you'll find in this neighborhood were built to house nobles and visiting royalty.

The Marais district, like many areas of town, has an ethnic quarter. If you're in search of a Jewish deli, this is the place.

SMART DINING

www.paris.org/Restaurants

Parisians love to eat, and they love to eat well. In fact, there are three times as many chefs in Paris as there are lawyers. Here, even the art of waiting tables is celebrated the **Garçon race**, in which hundreds of waiters race across town trying not to spill the drinks on their trays.

One of the best ways to eat in Paris—and certainly one of the most fun—is to build a meal from shop to shop the way many Parisians do. On the **Rue Cler**, not far from the Eiffel Tower, shops flow out onto the street, and the quality and selection of goods found there are outstanding. A charcuterie sells meat and some prepared foods, and you can pick up fresh fruits and vegetables at a *primeur*. Finally, stop at a nearby *pâtisserie* for a pastry.

When visiting Paris, at least one excellent meal is a must—and here it's possible even on a budget. One of my favorite places is **Les Bookinistes**, located in the Latin Quarter near the bookstalls on the Seine. A small, trendy restaurant, Les Bookinistes serves excellent food. Chef William LeDeuil is partnered with one of the most famous Parisian chefs, Guy Savoy.

Many of the city's elite chefs have opened small, less expensive restaurants that offer tourists a great way to taste fine French cuisine in an informal setting.

Cafés are the heartbeat of Paris. Like extensions of living rooms, cafés are where Parisians interact and exchange ideas. You'll find **Café de Flore** (**www.paris.org/Cafes/flore.html**) on Boulevard St. Germaine in the Left Bank. This is where artists, writers (Jean-Paul Sartre) and even the masterminds behind the French revolution hatched their greatest ideas.

The Metro

SMART TIP

To travel from site to site in Paris, look for the stylish red signs that indicate a Metro stop. A marvel of efficiency, the Metro is easy to figure out. Just study the map, pick your route and hop on. I usually buy a pack of 10 Metro tickets, a *carnet*. Then I don't have to wait in line and I always have tickets in case the ticket booth is closed. Feed the ticket through the turnstile; it'll pop up further along. Keep the ticket in a safe place— you never know when an inspector may ask to see it, and you'll be fined if you can't produce it. To change lines on the Metro, follow the signs that say "correspondence." To leave, look for "sortie" or "exit."

Wine bars are a wine lover's paradise. Unlike cafés, wine bars offer little-known, small-production wine by the glass, giving the connoisseur the chance to taste and discover new favorites. **Le Coude Fou** (12, rue du Bourg Tibourg), "crazy elbow," was named for the time-honored tradition of bending elbow and tipping back great wine. In this wine bar, you'll find a helpful staff and a great tasting selection.

Explore Paris

SMART TIP

Paris is a big city, but try to think of it as many little cities—each section is like its own village. Take some time to have coffee at the corner café, explore the shops and get a feel for wherever you're staying.

■ ■ ■ ■ # Provence

Tourism Web Site: www.provenceweb.fr

From the hot sun on your skin to the smell of fresh lavender and the sound of fountains splashing in a quaint square, Provence is a feast for the senses. The heart of this region is its land. Its sun-drenched fields, craggy mountain ranges and beautiful flowers will get under your skin and into your soul.

Provence is a large, diverse region, made up of villages clustered in *Vauclause*, *Bouches-du-Rhone*, *Var*, *Alpes-de-Haute Provence* and the *Alpes Maritimes*. The region derives its name from the Romans who conquered the area and named it Provincia Romana. When their fighting days were over, many Roman soldiers retired to their sunny province, where villages grew from the countryside or were built high atop craggy hills.

To make the most of your time in Provence, I recommend renting a car. While there are buses to some of the villages, your own car will allow you to explore charming villages that are off the beaten path. Be advised, however, that many villages don't allow cars—this means parking your car at the bottom of a hill and walking up to the village above. If you do rent a car, try to brush up on international driving signs and converting miles to kilometers.

To plan your trip, leaf through picture books like Jacobs and Palmer's *The Most Beautiful Villages of Provence* and choose the villages that interest you. Arm yourself with a Michelin guide and map. The opportunities are endless.

Speed Limits

SMART TIP

A kilometer is six-tenths of a mile, so you can just multiply by .6. For example, a speed limit of 80 kilometers translates to about 48 miles per hour.

St.-Remy-de-Provence

The Alpilles section of Provence is named for the nearby mountain range. If you're familiar with the work of Vincent van Gogh, you may feel like you've been here before. The craggy limestone mountains and landscape of cypress and olive trees infused the artist's work. This is van Gogh country.

Nestled at the base of the Alpilles Mountains is the town of St.-Remy-de-Provence. For centuries, poets, prophets and artists have found their way to this dreamy little town. But more than any other artist, van Gogh sought the essence of Provence.

In 1889, van Gogh committed himself to the asylum here after he cut off his ear in a fit of madness in the nearby city of Arles. He spent the year here and, in between his attacks, worked feverishly, producing 250 drawings and canvasses, among them some of his finest work. Van Gogh repeatedly painted the Alpilles Mountains, struggling to master the cypress and olive trees. Of the olive he wrote to his brother: "They are old silver, sometimes nearer blue, sometimes greenish...very difficult, very difficult. But that suits me."

Glanum

Some of the best-preserved Roman ruins in France are just south of St.-Remy in the ancient town of Glanum. The **Triumphal Arch**, with its sculpted reliefs of slaves and processions, commemorates Caesar's victories over the Gauls in what is now France. The mausoleum honors the grandsons of the Roman emperor Augustus. Both monuments were probably built in the first century.

Walking Path

SMART TIP

Alongside the asylum, there's a walking tour of the places van Gogh painted. A leaflet at the tourist office will show you the way.

Eygalieres

Deep in the heart of the Alpilles you'll find another Roman settlement, Eygalieres. Rising from a rocky hillside, Eygalieres is a picturesque village. Above part of the town is a hill crowned with the ruins of a castle that dates from the 12th century, a time of relative peace and prosperity. Many of the great castles, churches and abbeys in this region were built during this period.

THE SUNFLOWERS OF PROVENCE REACH THEIR PEAK IN LATE JUNE AND EARLY JULY, WHEN TEMPERATURES SOAR IN SOUTHERN FRANCE.

As small as it is, Eygalieres happens to have an elegant restaurant. **Chez Bru** prepares simple, traditional Provencal food in an intoxicating setting. Try one of their truffle dishes.

St. Sixte Chapel

Just outside of town, the 12th-century St. Sixte Chapel stands on the site of an ancient Roman temple dedicated to the spirit of the local spring. The chapel and cypresses appear to have been removed directly from a van Gogh painting.

Arles

The two big cities in central Provence are Arles and Avignon. Arles, the smaller of the two, is picturesque and charming—your typical Provence with an extraordinary history.

A couple of thousand years ago, Julius Caesar rewarded Arles for helping him defeat Marseilles by lavishing funds on the town, which soon became the capital of the Roman Empire in Provence—the Rome of the north.

Les Arenes

In its day, Les Arenes drew crowds of 20,000 Roman subjects to watch gladiators duel it out with wild beasts. Today the Arena still features bloody spectacles—though bulls and matadors have replaced the gladiators. You'll find two kinds of bullfights in Arles. The traditional Spanish-style, where the matador kills the bull, and the Provencal style, where it's the bullfighters who usually get hurt.

St. Trophime

The portal carvings in this 12th-century Romanesque church tell the story of the Last Judgment. In the depiction, the blessed, dressed in flowing robes, are led to heaven. The condemned, stark naked, are strung together by a chain and led to hell. The church's cloisters are also adorned with 12th-century art. The famous northwest pillars depict St. Trophimus, the first bishop of Arles in the third century. Perfume merchants are seated at the table. It's believed the stone used to build the church was cut from Arles' Roman ruins.

Avignon
www.avignon-et-provence.com

Avignon, central Provence's largest city, is about 25 miles north of Arles.

Papal Palace

In 1309, the Pope moved from Rome to Avignon to escape the political turmoil in Italy. For the next 70 years, a succession of popes lived lavishly in Avignon's Papal Palace. Today, the chambers and passages are largely barren, with hardly a hint of their former grandeur.

Pont St. Benezet

Partially crossing the Rhone River is the bridge made famous in the children's song "Sur le Pont d'Avignon," though today it is

Festivals

SMART TIP

All summer long, the villages of Provence throw festivals or parades. The festival in the town of Châteaurenard, for example, honors Saint Eloi, the patron saint of metal works and, by extension, all those who work with horses. Check this site for listings year-round: **www.franceguide.com/gb/franceFete/index.cfm.**

only half a pont. The raging Rhone river destroyed the bridge so many times that city leaders finally gave up their rebuilding and left it unrepaired in the 17th century. Still, the bridge offers a nice view back at the town.

Place de l'Horloge
Avignon is the artistic and cultural hub of Provence. Its summer arts festival draws a cosmopolitan crowd from all over Europe. During the festival, most of the action revolves around Avignon's main town square, Place de l'Horloge. Here you can choose from a dizzying number of cafés and restaurants.

Luberon
Mountainous and wooded, the Luberon area is named for its mountain range and known for its string of spectacular Provencal villages. To see its famed flowers in full bloom, time your visit for the summer months. Lavender begins to turn purple around the end of June and has usually been harvested by September.

Lavender oil is used for everything from perfume to a disinfectant. Due to the Roman habit of adding lavender to wash water, the word lavender is believed to come from the Latin word lavare, meaning "to wash."

Abbey of Senanque
One of the most striking places to get a lavender fix is the 12th-century Abbey of Senanque. The interior of the Abbey is simple and austere so that the monks would not be distracted by decoration. They rose for first service at 2 a.m. and spent much of their day copying manuscripts and meditating in the cloisters. The Abbey still functions as a Cistercian monastery. If you time your visit right, you might get a demonstration of the Abbey's acoustics.

If you're driving in Provence, you'll probably notice curious stone mounds sprinkled around the countryside. The borie are ancient stone dwellings. In the village of Borie, the dwellings have been restored. The stones are placed flat on top of one another with a downward slope. No mortar is used to hold them together.

Roussillon
All of the walls in this small town are red. Legend has it that the young wife of an evil lord fell in love with a troubadour. In a jealous rage, the lord killed the troubadour and served his wife the man's heart. When she discovered what she'd eaten, she threw herself off the cliffs, coloring them red with her blood. In fact, it is the ochre in the hillsides that has colored the town's walls red. For centuries, the townspeople mined the ochre for dye and pottery glaze. With the advent of synthetic dyes, however, Roussillon was forced to switch to tourism for its survival.

Open Mass

SMART TIP

At the Abbey of Senaque, mass is open to the public and sung in French Tues.–Sat. at noon and Sun. at 9 a.m.

THE TIME-PASSED VILLAGES OF THE LUBERON OFFER A PEACEFUL RETREAT FROM HECTIC BIG-CITY LIFE. RUDY SAYS, "RENT A CAR TO EXPLORE THESE PEACEFUL MOUNTAIN RETREATS."

Pont Julien

South of Roussillon sits yet another Roman engineering marvel, the Pont Julien. This bridge, which dates back to the third century, spanned a river on the Domitian Way—an ancient road that linked Italy to Spain. Remarkably, the bridge is still in use today.

Bonnieux

Set high on a hill overlooking the fields and farmland of Luberon, the charming town of Bonnieux feels like the top of the world. Here, the steep town streets are redolent with the smell of baking bread, and a sense of peace prevails.

Visit the Bonnieux cemetery, located just above the town, for breathtaking views of the surrounding countryside.

Aix-en-Provence
www.aixenprovencetourism.com

Aix, another town founded by Romans near a natural spring, is a vibrant university town with broad, tree-shaded avenues and hundreds of outdoor restaurants. The streets here are lively and the architecture elegant.

Seventeenth century mansions, once the residences of rich nobles, flank **Cours Mirabeau**, the city's main boulevard.

The light, color and vibrancy of this town inspired its most famous local resident—the father of modern art, Paul Cézanne. While there are few of Cézanne's paintings in Provence, a trip to his turn-of-the-century studio in Aix conjures up his presence.

Hiking Trails

SMART TIP

There are 37,000 miles of trails in France, some of which follow medieval paths from town to town. Cycling through Provence is a popular pastime. Be aware, however, that the summer months are hot. Use the many villages as steppingstones and travel in the cooler morning or evening hours.

In the summers, Cézanne would roam the countryside in and around Provence, painting Mont Saint Victoire from every angle and in every light. He was fascinated with how we see the world and used movement and color to simulate our constantly changing vision. In his later years, Cézanne turned to the art of still life, writing, "People imagine that things like a sugar bowl have no soul. But you have only to know how to treat them. They have to be coaxed, these little creatures, these glasses and fruit."

Today is Thursday and the weekly market in Aix is underway. Market day is like a fair, a riot of color and taste. The air is a heady mixture of coffee, lavender and spices. Here you can find an array of traditional Provencal cloth, try on hats or sample a luscious melon.

Cassis

The port town of Cassis is only about a 45-minute drive from Aix. An idyllic fishing port surrounded by vineyards and cliffs, Cassis lures with three kinds of bait: fabulous seafood, local wine and a trip to the Calanques, fjord-like bays surrounded by white cliffs.

Boat Tours

SMART TIP

Tour boats run frequently to these dramatic inlets surrounded by limestone cliffs. Adventurous souls can hike there or rent a motor-boat or kayak. Some boats stop for a swimming break at one of the three coves. Visit the local tourist office for schedules and packages.

FROM CASSIS, RUDY TAKES A BOAT TO INVESTIGATE THE CALANQUES, TALL WHITE CLIFFS THAT CREATE SOUTHERN FRANCE'S VERY OWN FJORD.

SMART DINING

Café de la Nuit, named for van Gogh's famous painting, *The Night Café*, is located in Arles' Place du Forum. Try the regional *pastis*, a potent licorice-flavored liquor.

Chez Bru (in Eygalieres) earned its Michelin star with simple, traditional Provencal food. For more information, e-mail **sbru@club-internet.fr**.

In Cassis, try *bouillabaisse*, a local treat. The murky broth and the assortment of fish are served separately. For dipping, try hard rounds of toast with garlic spread. Another local delicacy in the summer are big, juicy *moules*, or mussels. To accompany, an icy glass of rosé made from the grapes of Cassis grown on neighboring hills.

In Provence, truffles are known as black diamonds and are harvested from November to April. They have an earthy, almost nutty flavor. The truffle market in Carpentras runs from November to March on Fridays.

SMART LODGING

One way to let the flavor of Provence seep in is by staying in a small village. But be forewarned—early reservations are a must. I found a lovely country inn just north of St. Remy called La Maison. The inn sits atop a hill at the end of a dirt road. **www.lamaison-a-bournissac.com**

Markets

SMART TIP

Once a week, every village—large or small—has an outdoor market. Most guidebooks will tell you which day of the week a given town holds its market. If not, ask a local. This is a not-to-be-missed opportunity to peruse local specialties including coffee, lavender or spices. If you ask me, the best markets in Provence are the Thursday market in Aix and the Saturday market in Arles.

Secret Places

There aren't many secrets in the Provence region of the south of France. The subject of several best-selling books by English writer Peter Mayle, combed by guidebook authors, and a perennial favorite of American tourists, Provence is well mapped. But through sheer luck, I found a country inn with the sophisticated décor and cuisine of a four-star hotel. And because it opened only recently, it's not generally known. As far as I know, it is not yet listed in any guidebook.

Domaine de Bournissac is a 13-room, reasonably priced romantic hideaway at the end of a long, gravel road in the countryside not far from the village of Eyragues. It's only about a 10-minute drive from the larger town of St.-Remy, considered by many to be the heart of Provence. Guests find it's a quick drive to some of the prettiest spots in the region, such as the white cliffs of the perched village of Les Baux. In the countryside not far from Domaine de Bournissac, sunflower fields were in full bloom when I visited in early July. A bit farther north, fields of lavender basked in the warm summer sun.

There are many reasons first-time visitors to Provence fantasize about living there. Odds are, if you are lucky enough to stay at Domaine de Bournissac, part of your fantasy will be that your home will look exactly like the sitting rooms and guest rooms at Domaine de Bournissac. The centuries-old farmhouse that is the heart of the inn has been transformed by its owner—an interior designer who owns a fashionable restaurant in nearby Avignon—into a place of calm and tranquility. Furniture in muted earth tones, whites and grays gives the inn a cool, polished look. Natural wood and stone abounds. At night, candles are lit in the public areas and placed around the outdoor dining area.

I found the place because I'd called a well-regarded hotel in the area to book a room about six weeks before I intended to arrive. "I'm sorry, monsieur," said the voice on the other end of the phone, "but we are fully booked."

He suggested I call de Bournissac. I couldn't find it in my Michelin Guide, and said so. "Do not worry, monsieur; it is new, but I am certain you will find it to your liking."

That was an understatement. From the small parking lot, the façade of the stone farmhouse is simple, hardly suggesting the polished, understated design within. Down a few steps, surrounded by grass and overlooking acres of farm fields, a pool beckoned. A vegetable garden grows food for the *maison*. Growing next to the sidewalk to the front door is a rosemary I later learned the chef uses in his dinners.

Our room was spacious and spare, almost Asian in the cleanness of its design and décor. Huge bathrooms with oversized towels and sponge-painted walls welcomed us home every night after a day of visiting the countryside. We'd only planned to dine one night at the maison, but after our first night's dinner, there was no question this was a serious place for food, and we immediately booked for the next night. A nice selection of regional wines in the $30 range complement the kitchen's fresh dishes. Breakfasts are lavish spreads of fresh breads, fruits and juices. In the next year or so, the rest of the world will discover Domaine de Bournissac. Get there first.

Domaine de Bournissac
Montee d'Eyragues
13550 Paluds de Noves, France
Tel: (33) 4-90-90-25-25
Fax: (33) 4-90-90-25-26

Vacations France, a web-based clearinghouse for French rental homes, arranged for me to look at Mme. Vardi's farmhouse for my next trip. *Gites*—a loose term for everything from apartments to farmhouses—are a tradition with traveling Europeans. Most gites come with a kitchen and cooking utensils so you can cook your own meals. When gite-hunting on the Internet, choose web sites that offer lots of pictures and concrete information. **www.gites-de-france.fr** and **www.vacationsfrance.com**

■ ■ ■ ■ # Italy: Venice

Italian Tourist Web Guide: www.itwg.com/en_pisa.asp

Dining in Italy

SMART TIP

Italians take their food very seriously. If you're short on time, stand up in a *bar* and grab a panino or a *tramezzino*. Join the crowd for a cappuccino or an espresso. A *tavola calda* is like a delicatessen with meats and prepared foods—it's another great place for a quick, inexpensive snack or picnic lunch to go. If you order *un caffe* in Italy, you'll get an espresso. And you order your caffe in a bar. Keep in mind that if you sit down for your refreshment, you'll end up paying double for it. Traditionally, the *ristorante* is more elegant and expensive than other restaurants. A *trattoria* is more casual, with home-style cooking, and a *hostaria* is a local hangout with no menu. If you choose a restaurant that's off the beaten path, you're likely to get a better meal at a better price.

	VENICE
Official Tourism Web Site:	www.meetingvenice.it
Tourist Office:	Tourist Assistance
	Piazza San Marco
	Tel: 041-5226356

Magical, mysterious Venice—an enchanted place where sea becomes land, cars become boats, streets are canals and the lines between reality and fantasy quickly blur. The city's very existence defies reason. Built on mud flats and wooden stilts, it's a patchwork of land and sea. Yet this watery town became an empire and for 800 years grew in strength, wealth and pride.

From about 1100 through about 1600, merchants from all over the world met in Venice, known then as the Gateway to the East. And if Venice was the gateway to a continent, Piazza San Marco was the grand entryway to the city.

The winged lion is the symbol of Venice and nothing better represents Venetian tenacity, glory and pride.

Piazza San Marco

Remarkably, there may be more pigeons than tourists in Piazza San Marco. Locals claim that the birds that populate the piazza today are descendants of those released by the Doge every Palm Sunday.

Venice's original **Campanile**, or bell tower, collapsed in 1902. Fortunately, the only casualty was the caretaker's cat. Venetians completed the campanile you'll see during your visit in 1912. But don't worry; it's true to the original.

The gem of the piazza is the **Basilica of San Marco**, which looks as though it was taken directly from the pages of a fairy tale. When the interior of San Marco is illuminated, the mosaics sparkle—you may want to check in at the Basilica to find out the lighting schedule.

By the time the year 800 rolled around, Venice was still without a patron saint, so a couple of merchants took it upon themselves to steal the remains of Saint Mark from Alexandria, Egypt. To prevent Muslim customs officers from discovering their precious cargo, they hid the remains in a wicker basket of pork, which was certain to repulse the officers.

Once Saint Mark had arrived in Venice, merchants returning from their travels would stop at the Basilica to pay homage to their patron saint and to offer jewels or artwork they had picked up during their travels. The bronze horses over the main entrance are replicas of the ones stolen from Constantinople. For protection, the original horses are kept in a small museum upstairs in the Basilica. The museum is tiny and the only real artifacts are the horses, but that's enough!

Spend the Night

SMART TIP

A few hours in Venice aren't enough to do the city justice. Plan to spend at least a night so that you can explore the back streets and get away from the crowds. There are many hotels here, in every price range from palaces to canal-side pensiones—but no matter where you stay, reservations are a must. In the off season, which usually runs from about October to March, you can have the truly magical experience of having Venice all to yourself.

Plan Your Visit

The area around San Marco and the Rialto is fiercely touristed—if you'd like some breathing room, visit the area's markets and shops in the morning or in the evening. At midday, tour boats drop off thousands of tourists for sightseeing.

Grand Canal, Rialto and Mercerie

After paying homage to San Marco, merchants loaded their wares into smaller boats and set off down the Grand Canal, the closest thing you'll find in Venice to a main street.

Like set pieces in a fantasy film, lacy palaces line both sides of the Grand Canal. These palazzi were the homes of Venice's wealthiest merchants and carry the prefix "Ca'," which is short for casa, the Italian word for house. Early Venetians were an odd mix of the democratic and the tyrannical. The wealthy families elected their Doge and even put checks and balances on his power. At the same time, citizens regularly denounced each other to the secret police via complaints slipped through one of the many lions' mouths around the city.

Rich families in Venice were so competitive about displaying their wealth that "sumptuary laws" were passed to limit their competition with each other. Under the new laws, all gondolas were painted black, excessive finery in palaces was outlawed and a limit was even placed on the length of trains on women's dresses. Venetian women found a way to get around at least one of the laws. They began wearing enormous platform clogs so they could lengthen their dresses. The shoes were so high women needed the help of two escorts to stand.

Along the Grand Canal, in the heart of Venice's trading district, is the **Rialto Bridge**, once the meeting place for merchants from all over the world.

Just next to the bridge on the west side of the canal, you'll find the **Pesceria** and the **Erberia**, Venice's largest fish and produce markets, respectively. The alleys and quays around the markets are still named for the items traded in them.

The commercial district between the Rialto and San Marco is called the **Mercerie**. In the 1600s, a visitor to this area of Venice described it as full of "cloth of gold, rich damasks and other silks, perfumers, apothecaries and innumerable cages of nightingales." Today, many of the shops are overpriced tourist traps, but the color, life and energy of the market persists.

THE CAMPANILE, OR BELL TOWER, IN PIAZZA SAN MARCO COLLAPSED IN 1902. BY 1912 IT WAS COMPLETELY REBUILT AND STANDS TODAY AS ONE OF THE ENDURING SIGHTS OF VENICE.

Neighborhoods

Once you've visited the busy shops in and around Piazza San Marco and the Mercerie, escape the crowds in one of Venice's three neighborhoods, Dorsoduro, Cannaregio or San Polo.

In Italian, **Dorsoduro** means, literally, "hard back," so it makes sense that this is the largest spine of dry land in Venice. It's not too difficult to navigate Dorsoduro—stretching the length of the neighborhood is the **Zattere**, a long promenade and favorite strolling place of Venetians. When you've finished with your walk, detour to the **Accademia** for a look at Venice's fine collection of art. Dorsoduro is also home to one of Venice's liveliest meeting places, sunny **Campo Santa Margerita**. This neighborhood is also where you'll find the **Ponte di Pugni**, or "bridge of fists." Long ago, this bridge was the site of many battles between rival clan members.

Another neighborhood, **Cannaregio**, was originally called "regione delle canne" or "district of bamboo" after the marshland on which it was built. Unlike Dorsoduro with its upscale boutiques, Cannaregio offers visitors a look at working-class Venice. The back streets of this neighborhood, some of the loneliest in the city, offer a glimpse into how Venetians live.

Check out Cannaregio's exquisite church, the **Madonna dell'Orto**, which was named for a reputedly miracle-working statue of the Madonna found in a nearby garden.

Across the Grand Canal from Canareggio you'll find **San Polo**, one of the oldest and most atmospheric sections of Venice.

If you can, start your walking tour of this neighborhood from **Do Mori**, the city's oldest wine bar. In the afternoons, Venetians partake in the ritual of an *ombre*, a drink and a snack. One visit to Do Mori, and you'll learn to love this Venetian tradition.

San Polo is a mysterious maze of narrow streets and canals where you're bound to come upon sudden *campos* and hidden gardens. It is also where you'll find the grand 15th-century church **Chiesa dei Frari**. Dominating this superb church is the *Assumption of the Virgin*, a 16th-century work by the Venetian artistic superstar **Tiziano Vecellio**, known as Titian. The drama and bold colors of the *Assumption* startled and dismayed the friars who commissioned

The Traghetto

SMART TIP

There are only three bridges that cross the Grand Canal, so you'll have to take a *traghetto*, a ferryboat used mostly by the locals. The *traghetto* shuttles people across the canal regularly and, unlike more expensive gondola rides, should cost the equivalent of about 50 cents per ride.

The Vaporetto

SMART TIP

If you're planning to take your own trip down the Grand Canal, take a *vaporetto*, one of the local water buses. If you plan to take more than one trip, buy a one-, three- or seven-day pass at the ticket booth. If the stop where you board the vaporetto doesn't have a ticket booth, ask the boatman for a ticket or you might be fined.

the work in 1516. Chiesa dei Frari also houses **Giovanni Bellini**'s triptych *Madonna and the Saints*, a luminous example of Venetian Renaissance art. Bellini's use of perspective was so superb, this painting actually seems curved.

Lagoon Islands

Vaporettos and tour boats leave often from Piazza San Marco for the lagoon islands of **Murano**, **Burano** and **Torcello**. **Murano** is about a 15-minute ride, while Burano and Torcello are about 40 minutes away. Murano is famous for glass, which is tempting but difficult to carry home. If you must have some, the factories will ship, but it can be expensive.

In the 14th century, officials ordered the Venetian glassworks moved to Murano to lessen the fire danger in Venice proper and to guard the craftsmen's secret techniques. Woe to the artisan who tried to skip town—the glassmaking technique was so jealously guarded that errant glassmakers were hunted down and sometimes even executed.

Lace is to the small fishing village of **Burano**, the next island, as glass is to Murano. Some believe the delicate lace, which adorns shirts, tablecloths and doilies, is derived from a technique used to repair fishing nets. And it's a lot easier to transport home than glass.

As beautiful as the lace for which it is known are the colorful streets of Burano. Back when fishing was bigger than tourism, the women of Burano painted their houses in bright colors so their husbands could pick out their homes from the sea. Still today, residents of Burano are required to keep up the tradition by repainting their houses the same color every year.

THE ISLAND OF BURANO IS RENOWNED FOR LACE. RUDY AND HIS DAUGHTER SARAH STOCK UP ON LIGHTWEIGHT, "PACKABLE" SOUVENIRS. RUDY POINTS OUT VENETIAN LACE IS EASIER TO TRANSPORT THAN VENETIAN GLASS.

The most remote and wild of the islands is **Torcello**, the original site of Venice's earliest settlers. The highlight of your visit to Torcello will likely be its cathedral, which, built in 639 A.D., is Venice's oldest building. The simple interior of the cathedral on Torcello is adorned with splendid mosaics, including some from the 13th century that tell the story of the Last Judgment in vivid detail.

A series of wars and the loss of trade routes dealt a death blow to the Venetian Empire. The Venetian love of adventure turned to a love of gambling and parties—by the 18th century, Venice was Europe's party city. Carnival, the festival that's a last fling before Lent, lasted for months. Masks became a way of life—gamblers hid behind them, men and women flirted under their cover. People wore them so often that the clergy complained, insisting that masks should at least be removed in church.

Ca' Macana Mask Shop: **www.maskvenice.com**

SMART DINING

Venice can be a culinary treat but it also serves up plenty of mediocre, overpriced food. To get the most for your money, venture away from tourist areas and tourist menus. Explore the back streets of Venice to find an appealing out-of-the-way restaurant.

SMART TIP

Make a Reservation

If you have your mind set on a particular restaurant during high season, it's a good idea to book a table in advance.

Cantinone Storico
(s. vio Dorso Doro 660)
Great Venetian fare at reasonable prices.

Do Mori Wine Bar
(s. Polo 429) Stop in for a late-afternoon snack and glass of wine.

The specialty dessert of the region is *tiramisu*, layers of sponge cake, mascarpone, chocolate and coffee.

SMART LODGING

One of the finest, most beautiful hotels in the world is the **Cipriani**. Cipriani's luxurious accommodations, attentive service and fine cuisine offer its patrons a glimpse of Venetian hospitality at its best. The hotel is located on an island across from San Marco and away from the crowds. It has its own ferry to the mainland. Every day or evening, you get to enter Venice though the front door.
www.cipriani.orient-express.com

RUDY:
For la dolce vita at a reasonable price, I suggest visiting the convent/hotel **Casa Cardinal Piazza** in Venice—two elegant gray palazzi formerly occupied

by noble Venetian families. Located on a canal in the quiet, fashionable and historic district of Cannaregio, the Casa offers gracious hospitality in plain, modern guest rooms and large public rooms. Delicacies can be purchased in the small bakeries, delicatessens and wine shops that line the neighborhood's canals; feel free to take them to the convent's garden for a picnic.

Away from the hustle and bustle of San Marco, the Casa is an easy walk or vaporetto ride to all the marvelous sights and sounds of Venice. The convent has single and double beds, all with private bath. You can have breakfast at an additional cost, and half and full board are available upon request. Some English is spoken, and there is an 11 p.m. curfew. The least expensive way to reach the convent is to take water bus No. 52 and stop at Madonna dell'Orto.

The Gondola

SMART TIP

A gondola ride. It's part of the charm of Venice—but it's expensive, so why stick with the tourists? Get away from the gondola stations at San Marco and the Rialto and catch one at Campo Santa Maria Formosa, where the canals are quieter, smaller and more picturesque. Choose your gondolier and your route according to your tastes and negotiate the price before you start.

RUDY'S TIP FOR A MEMORABLE GONDOLA RIDE IS TO GET AWAY FROM THE TOURIST CROWDS AT SAN MARCO OR THE RIALTO BRIDGE, AND TO NEGOTIATE A PRICE AND A ROUTE BEFORE YOU BOARD. RUDY PREFERS THE QUIETER BACK CANALS FOR THE TRUE FLAVOR OF OLD VENICE.

▪ ▪ ▪ ▪ The Italian Riviera

From Genoa's historic port to Italy's most alluring resorts, the Italian Riviera is one of the most romantic places in the world. With its death-defying cliffs and beaches that glisten like jewels, this region of Italy offers as stunning a coastline as any you'll find in Europe. It was along this coastline that, centuries ago, Italy's small city-states made their fortunes thanks to prime waterfront real estate. Today, pastel fishing villages and shorelines radiate sunlight and offer a peaceful respite from densely populated cities filled with traffic and noise.

GENOA

Tourist Office: Via Roma 11/4
Tel: 010-541541
Fax: 010-581408

If you're looking for Old World elegance, a trip to Genoa is a must. The city, hugely popular with cruise ships, is busy and cosmopolitan. At first glance, Genoa looks like a typical sprawling city. But if you look past the modern facade, you'll find an Old World city that was once wealthy and grand. The sturdy walls that fortified Genoa are the second longest in the world next to the Great Wall of China. And they saw plenty of action. After the collapse of the Roman Empire, Italy fragmented into small city-states.

When Italian citizens weren't battling invaders from the rest of Europe, they were fighting among themselves. In the 13th century, Genoa engaged in fierce struggles with Venice and Pisa for domination of Mediterranean trade. Eventually, Genoa itself became a major maritime player.

Once you've arrived, head to the funicular station at **Largo della Zecca**. From here you can take the funicular up the hill for a view of the old city's fortresses. The narrow, winding streets that make up Genoa's historic center make exploring this part of the city on foot practically irresistible. The streets in this part of the city are closed to vehicular traffic.

Around every corner in Genoa, you'll be reminded that this was the birthplace of **Christopher Columbus**, without whom much of the gold seized by Spain from the New World would not have found its way back to this small town's harbor. Ironically,

Columbus' discovery of the New World, and the subsequent shift of international trade from the Mediterranean to the Americas, led to a decline in the city's wealth and status.

Cattedrale di San Lorenzo
In medieval times, Cattedrale di San Lorenzo was the heart of Genoa's political and religious life. As early as the 12th century, all of the city's major ceremonies, proclamations and elections happened here. During World War II, a British shell landed on the cathedral but miraculously failed to explode.

Find an Address

SMART TIP

Looking for an address in Genoa can be a little tricky. There are two sets of street numbers—red for commercial establishments and black for homes and office buildings.

The black slate and white marble that embellish the exterior and interior of the cathedral are very common in this part of Italy. Perhaps the most intriguing part of the cathedral is the **Chapel of John the Baptist**, which claims to hold not only John the Baptist's ashes, but also the plate on which his head was served to Salome and a chalice used during the Last Supper. San Lorenzo also houses numerous treasures seized from the Holy Land by medieval merchant sea captains.

Via Garibaldi
In the 16th century, Genoa's elite, flaunting their newfound wealth, built extravagant homes on what is now called Via Garibaldi. It was once known as "Golden Street." In just 10 years, 13 palaces were built here as Genoa's wealthiest families attempted to escape the cramped conditions in the town's center. Most of the palaces were complemented with expensive courtyards and colorful frescoes. Today, many of them have been converted into banks or galleries.

BLACK AND WHITE MARBLE ARCHES ARE TYPICAL OF MANY CATHEDRALS IN ITALY. THE CATTEDRALE DI SAN LORENZO IN GENOA IS A PRIME EXAMPLE.

Palazzo Reale

One of my favorite palaces, Palazzo Reale, is located just a few blocks off of Via Garibaldi. Today, its extravagant 17th-century Rococo rooms are used to display artwork. The palace was originally built as a home for the Balbis, a Genoese family that made its fortune in the silk trade. Later, Italian royalty purchased it.

A visit to the palace reveals a portrait of Caterina Balbi by Flemish painter **Anthony Van Dyck**, who was a close friend of the Balbi family. Much of the furniture is preserved from Genoa's golden age, a glimpse into the style to which the city's aristocracy had become accustomed. The ballroom on the upper floor is especially decadent and the mirrored gallery should look familiar to Francophiles—it was modeled after the Hall of Mirrors at Versailles.

Portofino

Nineteenth-century artists were drawn to the unparalleled beauty of Portofino, and it's no wonder. This small port just south of Genoa is as romantic as a picture postcard. Once upon a time, Hollywood types like Ingrid Bergman and Humphrey Bogart would come here to escape the prying lenses of the paparazzi. Today, however, Portofino is far from private. Day-tripping tourists prowl the streets and the small harbor is like a club for international chic. The town square is perfect for sipping an espresso and people-watching.

Cinque Terre
www.cinqueterre.it

Cinque Terre, which means "five lands," is a string of five fishing villages hidden between the mountains and the sea on the cliffs just south of Portofino. If you're craving glorious scenery and serious relaxation, Cinque Terre is the place for you. Stretched along a 15-mile span of the coast, the cliffs of Cinque Terre look like giant staircases of terraced vineyards and olive groves. Locals insist that the best olive oil in Italy comes from these hills.

Years ago, you could reach the towns of Cinque Terre only by donkey or boat. Now, a commuter train delivers passengers to each of the towns daily, and the old donkey paths have become a hiker's paradise.

Monterosso al Mare

Located at the northernmost point of the Cinque Terre, Monterosso is the only one of the villages accessible by car. You can take a taxi into town, but private vehicles are restricted. Because of its accessibility, Monterosso is more touristed than the other towns and there is an abundance of hotels and restaurants.

The main town is divided into new and old sections by a medieval tower adorned with a rose window. Before it was overshadowed by big trading cities like Genoa and Pisa, the Cinque Terre saw its share of prosperity. It was considered a status symbol for a town to be able to afford a rose window.

Tour Boats

SMART TIP

Genoa's fortunes have always been linked to the sea. I recommend hopping aboard one of the city's tour boats to see the waterfront and hard-working harbor. Harbor tours leave daily from Porto Antico on the waterfront.

Vernazza is one of five villages of the Cinque Terre on the Italian Riviera, 45 minutes south of Genoa by train. Rudy suggests saving time to hike between the villages.

For the most part, the Cinque Terre doesn't offer the expansive beaches for which the big resort areas of the Riviera are known. Most of the beaches here are more pebbly than sandy but are still great for swimming. Monterosso's sandy beach is probably the best you'll find among the five villages.

Vernazza

Vernazza is about an hour-and-a-half by foot from Monterosso, or a moment's train ride. Blessed with a rocky spit, it is the only one of the five towns with a real port. The old tower that rises above the town remains from the days when Turks and pirates terrorized the coast, sometimes kidnapping residents and selling them into slavery in the East.

Corniglia

Unlike the other Cinque Terre towns, Corniglia is perched on a hillside far above a stretch of rocky beach. The town is home to about 250 people. In the evenings, you'll find everyone in the main square gossiping about the day's activities and chatting with passersby.

Commuter Train

SMART TIP

You can buy a special train ticket that allows you unlimited travel between each of the villages. By train, each town is only minutes from the next, so the passes can really come in handy. If you decide to hike through the Cinque Terre, you should be able to pass through each of the villages in about five hours. If this is your preference, remember to ask about the status of the trail you choose. The paths are often closed for maintenance and improvements.

On the road from Corniglia to Manarola you'll find the Cinque Terre's wine co-op. The winemaking tradition here dates back to Roman times. In fact, a wine jug from Corniglia was found among the ruins at Pompeii. The sweet white wine for which this region is known is made only with grapes grown near the sea. In the old days, the wine was used as a medicine or brought out to celebrate a wedding or a birth. Today, it's prized as a dessert wine.

Manarola
Just down the coast from Corniglia lies Manarola, a quaint fishing village that clings like a barnacle to a dark, rocky cliff. Each morning, fishermen set out in colorful boats as their ancestors have done for centuries. In the evening, lucky diners reap the rewards of the day's catch.

Riomaggiore
Time to get out the cameras. This village puts the picture in picturesque. Riomaggiore, the southernmost town in the Cinque Terre, is a beehive of peeling pastel houses and lively cafés. According to tradition, the village was founded in the eighth century by a group of Greek refugees who were fleeing religious persecution. Today, the town still welcomes those seeking refuge. If you're interested in renting a room in a private Italian home, there are plenty of options here.

Short Hike

SMART TIP

For a short hike, take the most popular trail in the Cinque Terre. The 20-minute trek from Manarola to Riomaggiore is known as Via dell'Amore or "trail of love."

FROM RUDY MAXA'S TRAVELER NEWSLETTER

Making the Most of Your Camera Abroad

After a summer of watching tourists photograph Europe, I came up with four rules for taking good pictures.

I spent a good part of my summer in Europe hosting **Smart Travels** for public television, and I can tell you the single, overwhelming impression I brought home: Tourists don't know how to take pictures.

Almost all my time was spent at classic tourist locations. And time and again, I'd watch men and women point their cameras in ways that almost guaranteed they'd be disappointed when their film was developed. Here are three basic truths about photography:

- If you shoot into the sun, you'll almost always wind up with an overexposed picture.

- If you try to get the entire facade of Buckingham Palace in your frame with your spouse or best friend standing in front, your spouse or best friend will appear pin-like in the resulting photo.

- A flash bulb cannot illuminate the Eiffel Tower or one of the great pyramids of Giza at night.

Small 35-mm cameras as well as hand-held video cameras have grown increasingly sophisticated, but all the smart chips and savvy electronics cannot compensate for plain, old bad photography. And that holds true for digital cameras, as well—though at least with a digital camera you know right away if you've taken a bad picture, and you can erase it and try again.

Now, you do not have to be a professional photographer to produce pictures that you, friends and family members will enjoy seeing later. While I did some freelance photography in college and have had photos published in major magazines, I'm no expert. But I've interviewed a dozen photographers about the most common mistakes we amateurs make. Below is an abbreviated version of their most useful advice; see if you can't improve your snaps next time you're on the road.

The Basics
- Always fill the frame with the heart of the picture. If you're shooting someone standing in a field of sunflower blossoms, you don't need the upper half of the photo to be sky. (Unless it's a spectacular sky!) Fill the frame with your subject and the brilliant blossoms. Before you release the shutter, imagine the photo as a whole and cut out anything superfluous by coming in closer on the subject.

- A flash bulb can only illuminate subjects from 6 to 10 feet away. It won't illuminate Michelangelo's statue of Saint Peter in the basement of the Duomo in Amalfi—or the Roman Colosseum at night.

- Always try to have natural light falling across the front of your subject. Dappled sunlight usually doesn't work well. If you're in brilliant light, fill in the subject by using a flash; that's called "fill flash," and it makes your subject "pop" out of the bright background.

- If you want rich, warm colors, shoot early in the morning or as the sun goes down.

THE FIELD OF MIRACLES IS THE SITE OF PISA'S DUOMO AND THE FAMOUS "TIPSY TOWER".

PISA
www.itwg.com/en_pisa.asp

Tourist Office: Via B. Croce 26
                        56125 Pisa
                        Tel: 011-39-050-40202
                        Fax: 011-39-050-40903

In the Middle Ages, Pisa was a maritime powerhouse and, like people in other affluent Italian towns of the time, its citizens poured money into architectural and religious wonders.

Leaning Tower
http://torre.duomo.pisa.it

The **Leaning Tower of Pisa** is probably the most recognizable monument this side of the Eiffel Tower and is one of three grand structures in Pisa's Field of Miracles. Erected on water-soaked clay rather than a solid foundation, the tower began to lean after only three stories had been built, and construction was halted. Undeterred by the unstable foundation, the Pisans finished the eight-story marble tower a century later. While there are ongoing efforts to stabilize the tower, its tilt continues to increase about a millimeter a year. The building was designed as a bell tower for the Duomo, a very influential building in its day.

Duomo

The distinctive Romanesque style of Pisa's **Duomo**, with its dark and light stripes and blind arches, was imitated across Italy. The dome's haunting interior was a perk offered by the city's former domination of this part of the Mediterranean. When Pisa's powerful fleet drove the Muslim Turks from Sicily, they captured a treasure trove of riches for their trouble and invested their fortune in a cathedral that would stand as a symbol of the victory of Christianity over Islam.

Many visitors to Pisa's famous tower overlook the indoor cemetery next to the Duomo. Legend holds that during the crusades, 10 Pisan ships carried soil from Calvary in the Holy Land and laid it here in this cemetery. The frescoes that adorn the cemetery walls were among the largest in Europe before they were damaged by fire in World War II. The massive chains that hang on the wall were once used to close access to Pisa's harbor.

> *When the Genoese defeated the Pisans, they took away the chains to Genoa and gave half of the chain to its ally, Florence. Many centuries later, the chains were returned to Pisa by the two cities as a sign of friendship.*

Baptistery

The nearby Bapistery is like an enormous Romanesque crown topped by lacy Gothic gables and statuary. Sculptor **Nicola Pisano** designed its beautiful hexagonal pulpit, which rests on the backs of three marble lions. Some claim that the Renaissance started with Pisano's work here. The *Naked Hercules* represented a move away from the medieval sensibility and a return to the classics.

SMART DINING

If you visit the Cinque Terre, follow your nose to a local bakery for *focaccia al formaggio*, a pizza-like bread with cheese. It's simply scrumptious.

Ristorante Rosa (Via Ruffini 11) is a few miles from Portofino in the town of **Camogli**. The locals recommend the pesto, made with parmesan, pine nuts, olive oil and basil fresh from the garden. Be sure to save room for dessert.

Splendido Mare: www.hotelsplendido.net – restaurant at Hotel Splendido

SMART LODGING

If you're in the mood to indulge in starry-eyed luxury, stay at Portofino's **Hotel Splendido**. Perched on a hilltop, the hotel offers spectacular suites and balconies overlooking the town's harbor. Originally built as a monastery in the Middle Ages, Splendido looks more like a film set from the Jazz Age. Unless money is no object, this is the kind of place you'll probably want to save for that "special occasion."

Hotel Splendido: www.hotelsplendido.net – Portofino

Hotel Cinque Terre: www.cinqueterre.net/ostello – Manarola

Hotel di Stefano: www.hoteldistefano.pisa.it – Pisa

■ ■ ■ ■   The Hill Towns of Tuscany and Umbria

Tourism Web Site: www.umbrialink.com

Tourist Office in
Region of Umbria: Via Mazzini 21
06100 Perugia
Tel: 011-39-075-572-5341
Fax: 011-39-075-573-6828

Like variations on a phrase of music, the hill towns of Umbria and Tuscany follow a similar pattern, yet each is unique. Their valleys, replete with vineyards and olive trees, give way to medieval castles that transport the traveler to another time.

In medieval times, when these towns were built, life was short; food and possessions were scarce. Peasants worked in the fields below the villages, trudging up the hill at the end of the day to take comfort within their walled towns. For the rich, however, the walls offered little comfort. Mighty families spent their days consolidating their power and prestige by seeing who could build the most and tallest towers.

Today, the hill towns still celebrate food, saints, wine and ancient victories all summer long. These celebrations offer unique insights into the life and culture of Tuscany and Umbria. Seek them out! Ask at your hotel or at the local tourist office.

San Gimignano
www.sangimignano.com
For the best look possible at medieval Tuscany, pay a visit to San Gimignano. From a distance, this well-preserved hill town appears to have a modern skyline. In its heyday, San Gimignano boasted some 70 towers. Today, only 14 remain.

There were two main rival families in San Gimignano—the Salvucci and the Ardinghelli. If you were allied with the Salvucci and you walked under an Ardinghelli tower, there was a good chance you might be covered in boiling oil or bombarded with stones. If the cry came from a watchman that a neighboring town was invading, however, bad blood was forgotten and feuding families banded together to fight. Some experts believe that these towers were connected together with footbridges. In times of trouble, the villagers could use the footbridges as an alternative to the streets below.

Today, San Gimignano locals may wish it were that easy to escape the hoards of tourists who invade their community daily. To truly enjoy this town, arrive early, stay late, or

FOURTEEN MEDIEVAL TOWERS STILL DOMINATE THE SKYLINE OF SAN GIMIGNANO. IN THE MIDDLE AGES, DURING SAN GIMIGNANO'S HEYDAY, RICH FAMILIES COMPETED WITH EACH OTHER TO BUILD THE TALLEST AND BEST TOWERS.

settle into one of the local hotels. If you'd like to avoid the crowds altogether, visit San Gimignano in the off season.

Siena
www.sienanet.it
Twenty-five miles southeast of San Gimignano, Siena follows the hill town blueprint, but on a much larger scale.

The town's size gives it another level of loyalties and rivalries, dividing Siena into 17 districts or *contrade*. Each *contrada* is known by an animal symbol that reflects one of the 17 virtues of Siena. During your trip, you'll see the contrade plaques and flags all over town.

Palio
Today, the rivalries among the contrade are played out in Il Campo, Siena's central *piazza*. **The Palio** pits contrada against contrada in a wild bareback horse race that loops three times around the square. The Palio takes place twice a year on July 2nd and August 16th, but you don't have to visit during the festival to get a feel for the event. Year-round, you'll find the contrade doing something to prepare for the event.

Each contrada keeps a museum that is dedicated to the Palio. The museums are often open to the public around the time of the race or by appointment through the tourist office.

Avoid the Crowds

SMART TIP

To avoid huge crowds, catch the trial horse racing three days before the Palio. Then watch the official Palio on television.

Book in Advance
It's no secret that Siena's a great place to visit. Booking a room in advance—especially around the time of the Palio—is always a good idea.

Duomo

Each hill town takes great pride in its cathedral, or *duomo*, and Siena is no exception. In the 14th century, Siena planned a massive cathedral that would dwarf Florence's cathedral, but in the planning stages a plague struck and the church you see today is only a fraction of what it might have been. Still, Siena's lavishly ornamented **Duomo** is dazzling.

But it's not this cathedral's unique style of architecture that makes Sienans most proud. The floor of the cathedral is the true artistic treasure. It took some of Siena's best artists more than three centuries to complete. Inlaid with marble imported from the Orient, the floor panels tell biblical as well as mythological stories.

Siena and Florence were deadly enemies. But they were deadly enemies for centuries. Evidence of their fierce rivalry can still be seen today in Siena's **Palazzo Pubblico** and the tower next door, **Torre di Mangia**. Both the piazza and the tower were built to surpass their Florentine counterparts.

Like Florence, Siena made its fortune through trade and banking. To get a sense of how the wealthy lived, visit the palaces on the streets of Via Di Citta and Via Bianchi di Sopra.

Val D'Orcia

Heading south from Siena, we are in the region of Val d'Orcia, known for great Italian wines, moldering castles and mystic abbeys. Here you can find lesser-known hill towns and a view of life as it has been lived in the region for thousands of years.

Montalcino

Montalcino is the only place where *Brunello*, a deep red wine, is produced. In this sleepy town, the rich ruby treasure is plentiful in every *trattoria* and café. To taste some of the best Brunello this area has to offer, head to **Castello Banfi**. The Banfi estate, which is run by two American importers, is located in an 11th-century castle atop a hill just south of Montalcino. **www.castellobanfi.com**

SOUTH OF SIENA, THE VAL D' ORCIA ENCHANTS WITH UNDULATING HILLS, ROWS OF CYPRESS TREES AND OF COURSE, ITS VINEYARDS.

Brunello, like its rival, Chianti, is based on the Sangiovese grape. Sangiovese literally means the blood of Jove or Jupiter, the supreme deity of the ancient Romans. Brunello is considered one of the best wines produced in Italy today.

Not far from Montalcino, nestled among olive and cypress trees, is the **Abbey of Sant'Antimo**. Legend claims that Charlemagne founded the first abbey here in the eighth century. If you come on Sunday, you are likely to hear the haunting Gregorian chants for which these musical monks are known.

Orvieto

Built high on a volcanic outcropping in the province of Umbria, Orvieto is one of the few hill towns that didn't need walls for protection. The town is smaller and more remote than Siena, but the streets are charming.

Lorenzo Maitani, a master architect from Siena, designed Orvieto's 14th-century **Duomo**, the pride of the city. The interior of the Duomo is known for the Signorelli frescoes in the San Brizio chapel. In them, the 16th-century artist tells the story of the Creation through the Last Judgment in sometimes horrifying detail. Signorelli peopled his scenes with contemporaries, including his ex-girlfriend, whom he places on the back of a flying devil. If you have time, cross the street to the **Hotel Maitani**, named for the architect. The 16th-century *palazzo* Maitani is one of the best of its kind.

Beneath the medieval streets of Orvieto lie underground passages that once were part of the ancient city of Volsinii, one of the largest of many ruins in this area. In the seventh century B.C., Volsinii was a great city peopled by the Etruscans, for which Tuscany was named.

Take a Tour

SMART TIP

Tours of the underground city leave from the tourist office every day.

To truly appreciate Orvieto and its ruins, it helps to have a general knowledge of this ancient race of people. For a quick review, head to the **Museo "Claudio Faina,"** a private collection of Etruscan treasures.

There are a few Etruscan tombs just outside of Orvieto, but a longer drive takes you to a lonely necropolis and a string of hill towns in southern Tuscany.

The Etruscans are clouded in mystery. Their origin is unclear. No written texts from their civilization remain. Most of what we know about the Etruscans comes from their tombs. Etruscans preferred peace to war; they loved the good life—wine, food, music. Etruscan women enjoyed an equality and freedom that shocked and scandalized both the Greeks and Romans of the time. From the seventh century B.C. to their defeat by the Romans in the third century B.C., these mystical, life-loving people thrived. Tuscany bears their name.

FLAG-TWIRLING COMPETITIONS ARE REGULAR SUMMERTIME EVENTS IN THE
MANY SMALL VILLAGES THAT DOT THE TUSCAN COUNTRYSIDE.
FOR BEHIND-THE-SCENES VIEWS OF LIFE IN THE HILL TOWNS, RUDY TELLS
TRAVELERS TO SEEK OUT LOCAL FESTIVALS AND CELEBRATIONS LIKE THIS.

Pitigliano

Pitigliano, ancient, quiet and undisturbed by masses of tourists, grows straight out of
the volcanic tufa hill on which it sits. In the 17th century, a Jewish community took refuge
here from persecution in the Papal states. Today, the streets are quiet.

The volcanic hillside is riddled with caves that were excavated by the Etruscans. The
caves are still used today for storing wine and olive oil. Stop in at a local trattoria to
sample the local specialty—wild boar and wine.

Sovana

Just northwest of Pitigliano near the town of
Sovana is another series of Etruscan roads and
tombs. While these aren't the most dramatic
Etruscan tombs in Italy, they are some of the
loneliest and most evocative. Sunken roads,
some 30 feet deep, are thought to have been
used for funeral processions.

The **Tomba della Sirena**, with its eroded
mermaid relief, and the **Tomba Ildebranda**
with a Greek-style colonnade, are two of
the more impressive examples of Etruscan
ruins in this area.

Assisi
www.assisi.com

North of these ruins, in the heart of Umbria,
is Assisi, birthplace of Francesco Bernardone,
known to most as St. Francis. Each year, a
reported five million tourists and pilgrims flock
to this pink and gray hill town.

Parking

SMART TIP

When you stay in the center
of a hill town like Assisi,
drive to your hotel to drop
off your bags and check in.
The hotel staff will then
direct you to overnight parking. Navigating the streets
can be frustrating.
As you enter town, look for
signs directing you to the
hotels. Then be patient and
learn to recognize the ***Do Not
Enter*** signs—many streets are
one way.

Born the son of a wealthy merchant in 1182, Francis was an outgoing and cheerful youth. His friends named him the King of Revelers, for he loved parties, feasts and fun. Raised on notions of chivalry and honor, he longed to be a knight. In his first battle as a knight with neighboring town Perugia, Francis was captured. He spent a miserable year in a cold, damp prison. It was after this experience that Francis—much to his father's dismay—began to give away his clothes and money to the poor. Having heard the word of God, Francis renounced all earthly possessions in front of his angry father and the Bishop of Assisi. He never took holy orders and knew little of church doctrine; instead he wandered the countryside preaching a simple message of love, poverty and compassion. After the doom-and-gloom sermons the people were accustomed to, St. Francis's simplicity and charismatic joy came as a surprise and a relief.

Assisi's two-storied **Basilica di San Francesco**, named for the patron saint, is a grand reminder of a simple life. The *upper church* contains a series of frescoes attributed to the artist Giotto and his pupils around the year 1290. The frescoes, nearly destroyed in an earthquake in 1997, have since been restored. It's worth noting that many Italians question whether Giotto painted all of the frescoes.

With its dark vaults, the *lower church* gives off a somber feeling. Fearing that the Perugians would steal their saint's body, the early Franciscans hid St. Francis' tomb behind tons of stone. The saint's remains now rest above the altar. In the lower church, pilgrims of all ages and nationalities pay their respects to St. Francis.

Gubbio

Just north of Assisi sits Gubbio. Legend has it that St. Francis saved the town from a vicious wolf by bargaining with it. Behave yourself, Francis told the wolf, and the townspeople will feed you. Legend has it the tamed wolf became popular in this pretty hill town.

Apart from its pet wolf, Gubbio is known for its tradition of colorful ceramics. The discovery of blue and yellow glazes in the 15th century and the influence of designs by Spanish moors combined in the ceramic art called *majolica*. The art of Italian majolica flourished in the Renaissance. In the 16th century, Gubbio's master potter, Mastro Giorgio, invented a ruby red glaze that made him famous. He guarded the secret so jealously, however, that he took it to his grave. Not until this century was his secret rediscovered. Check out Leo Grilli's majolica shop at Via dei Consoli, 83.

SMART DINING

The winery at the Banfi estate offers a daily tour, showing how the grapes are grown in and around Montalcino, the types of casks used and how to tell a good Brunello from a mediocre one. The tour includes a lesson in winemaking and a tasting. At the end, you can test (and taste) your knowledge over a delicious meal at Banfi's restaurant. **www.castellobanfi.com**

SMART LODGING

Hotel Maitani: www.argoweb.it/hotel_maitani

Park Hotel ai Cappuccini: www.parkhotelaicappuccini.it - former convent

RUDY:

Far from the sea, in the hills of Umbria, you'll find a guesthouse run by Dominican sisters in the captivating medieval town of Orvieto. Steps away from the bustling Piazza del Popolo, the rather drab building of the **Istituto Santissimo Salvatore** belies the convenience, comfort and hospitality found within. Just a short walk away is a famous 13th-century Gothic cathedral. The soaring, seven-foot-high façade of this duomo is one of the most magnificently decorated in Europe. And the town itself is filled with quaint restaurants and shops that sell the fine white wines for which this Etruscan hill town is famous. The sisters have single and double rooms, all with private baths. Half board is available and the curfew is 10:30 p.m. Pay parking can be found in the old town very near the convent.

Stay the Night

SMART TIP

During the summer, Assisi can be crowded and overly commercial. My tip: try staying the night in Assisi. Early in the morning or late at night, when the crowds vanish, time rolls back several centuries.

Florence

Tourism Web Site: www.english.firenze.net

Tourist Office: Via Manzoni 16
50121 Firenze
Tel: 011-39-055-23320
Fax: 011-39-055-234-6286

In the 14th and 15th centuries, an electric combination of enterprise, wealth and a growing sense of the power of the individual created an explosion of thought called the **Renaissance**. Confidence, pride and a thirst for knowledge so great that it changed the course of history: Florence isn't just another small city in Italy, Florence gave birth to the modern world.

A trip to this Tuscan town is like a trip to another time. Behind the sublime architecture and dazzling art loom the great personalities that shaped the Renaissance. Most were contemporaries and many friends whose rivalries and collaborations drove art to extraordinary heights.

From the collapse of the Roman Empire in the 5th century until approximately the 14th century, Europe struggled through the Middle Ages. Barbarians regularly pillaged towns, brutal battles were fought between independent city-states, and disease, starvation and poverty were a part of everyday life. During that time, the only institution that prevailed was the Catholic Church, which offered believers the consolation that this life was merely a preamble to the glory of heaven. By the 13th century, however, Florentine trade had made the city's citizens the wealthiest in Italy. In fact, the city was wealthier than most countries. This newfound wealth gave the Florentines confidence, a concept that, while very new to them, allowed them to shift their focus from life after death to life in the here and now, from the divine to man. This new way of life demanded a new philosophy, which they found in their ancestors, the Greeks and Romans. Henceforth, all things Florentine reflected their new ideals: beauty, the grandeur of the human form, pride, confidence and invincibility.

The miracle of the Renaissance is still very much alive in our society today. In fact, many tenets of the Western world were born—or born again—in Florence. Our philosophy, our desire to excel and our belief in the power of the individual were all closely held beliefs during the Renaissance.

Florence is hot, overcrowded and can be overwhelming. My advice is to come prepared. To really enjoy yourself, have an idea of what you'd like to see this trip and what you're willing to save for next time.

Reading

SMART TIP

To learn more about Renaissance artists, read *Lives of the Artists* by Giorgio Vasari.

Markets

Before you visit one of Florence's many museums, I recommend getting a feel for the city and its history in one of its markets. **Mercato Nuovo** is located near the Arno River, where the dark back streets and alleys still evoke the Middle Ages. **Mercato Centrale** is Florence's largest and most entertaining market. In this market you'll find most of the leather goods for which Florence is famous, though quality varies. It's possible you'll find a lot of junk here, but you'll also find plenty of life.

Florentines have been holding markets for centuries. Mercato Nuovo has been held in Florence since the 11th century. It was markets like Mercato Nuovo, rich in commerce and trade, that helped lift the gloom of the Middle Ages. When Italian merchants opened trade routes to the East, money and new ideas flowed into Europe. During the Renaissance, Florence specialized in textiles, importing wool and exotic dyes and exporting cloth.

Via Tournabuoni

Florence is Italy's biggest fashion center after Milan. Take a stroll down **Via Tournabuoni** to get a feel for the way chic Florentines live today. At the end of the street, you'll find yourself in Medici country.

The Medici family capitalized on the success of the textile industry and became bankers, modern-day financiers and moneylenders. First Cosimo de Medici, and then his grandson Lorenzo the Magnificent, ruled Florence from behind the scenes and spent lavishly on the arts. Lorenzo opened a school for sculptors and painters in his garden. One day, he discovered a boy with exceptional talent and invited him to live at the Medici palace. His name was Michelangelo and Lorenzo raised him like a son. From the 14th to 18th centuries, members of the Medici family married into the major houses of Europe and rose to prominence as the family that would shape the destiny of Florence.

Bargello
www.arca.net/db/musei/bargello.htm

The National Museum, **Bargello**, houses the sculptural treasures of **Donatello**, one of the first sculptors to adopt the new philosophies of the Renaissance. In his work,

Donatello looked to the art of the past, that of the Greeks and Romans, for inspiration. He visited Rome to study and measure the ancient statues being uncovered there, bewildering the Romans who thought him a treasure hunter.

Donatello's bronze statue of *David* was the first freestanding nude since antiquity, yet the statue is by no means a copy of the ancients. The grace, individuality and palpable shyness of the boy make Donatello's statue distinctly modern.

To our eyes, there is nothing so revolutionary about these statues of individual men. But to the citizens of Florence, they were astonishing. The realism of the human form, the individuality of the features, and the emotions expressed were all breathtakingly new.

The Accademia

The Renaissance is said to have culminated in one work of art: *David* by Michelangelo. Found in Florence's Accademia Gallery, the work was carved from an enormous block of marble by Michelangelo when he was only 25 years old and was believed to symbolize the Florentine determination to defend its freedom—no matter how imposing its enemies.

> David *was carved from a huge leftover piece of ruined marble. When it was completed, the mayor of Florence admired the statue, but complained to the artist that the nose was too big. Michelangelo grabbed his chisel and scooped up a handful of marble dust. He climbed to the nose, pretended to chisel and let the dust fall. "Much better," the mayor exclaimed. "It really comes to life now."* David *went on, nose and all, to become the most celebrated statue of all time.*

The Accademia also houses the *Slaves*, Michelangelo's unfinished masterpieces. Aptly titled, the slaves appear to be trying to struggle free of their marble prisons. Michelangelo believed that his sculptures already existed within the stone; it was just a matter of setting them free.

DAVID BY MICHELANGELO IS THE MOST FAMOUS SCULPTURE OF ALL TIME AND A HIGHLIGHT OF ANY VISIT TO FLORENCE.

The Baptistery

The wealthier Florence grew, the more the citizens yearned to express their newfound prestige with art. In 1401, the wool importers' guild announced a contest—an artist would be chosen to design the north doors of the city's Baptistery. An artist named **Ghilberti** won the day and 48 years later he completed both the north and the now more famous east doors, which contain a self-portrait of the artist. Michelangelo is said to have gazed in awe at the work on the east doors and named them the *Gates of Paradise*. The door panels you see on the Baptistery today are copies. Ghilberti's original doors are in the **Museo dell'Opera del Duomo**.

Duomo

Just across from the Baptistery is the cathedral of Florence, the **Duomo**. The dome, designed by Filippo Brunelleschi, is the cathedral's crowning masterpiece—a glorious, elongated architectural wonder that is shaped a lot like an egg.

In 1420, a competition was underway in Florence to build a dome on its unfinished cathedral. A committee of architects and officials were gathered around a table, arguing about how it could be done. No one had built a dome this big since the ancient Romans. One of the architects, Brunelleschi, passed an egg around. "Make it stand on end," he told them. Everyone tried and failed. When the egg came back to Brunelleschi, he crushed the tip of the egg on the table, making it stand on end. The other artists scoffed. "We could have done that," they said. "Yes, but you didn't," Brunelleschi replied. He got the job.

The confidence and bravado of the Florentines was legendary. The Pope once said of Brunelleschi that he would be brave enough to turn the world over on its axis. "Just give me a point, Your Holiness, where I can fix my lever, and I'll show you what I can do," the artist answered.

THE DUOMO AND GIOTTO'S TOWER DOMINATE ONE OF FLORENCE'S MAIN SQUARES.

The painter and architect Giotto designed the bell tower next to the cathedral 80 years before Brunelleschi designed the Duomo. When asked for a sample of his work, Giotto reportedly drew a perfect circle in freehand. The point—geniuses don't submit samples.

Oltrarno

Across the Arno River from Florence's center is an area of town known as the Oltrarno. To get there, you must cross the **Ponte Vecchio**.

Climb the Tower

SMART TIP

The climb up Giotto's tower is difficult, but the view from the top allows you to survey all of Florence and gaze down onto Brunelleschi's masterpiece.

In 1345, when the Ponte Vecchio was built, butchers, blacksmiths and tanners crowded it. After a couple of hundred years, the ruler of Florence took a walk across the bridge and found the sights and smells repulsive. He evicted them all and allowed only goldsmiths on the bridge—where they remain today.

The Oltrarno is quieter and even seems cooler than the rest of Florence. Cafés and trendy restaurants line the streets and squares. In little shops and workrooms, artisans continue a tradition of carving, gilding and restoring that is unparalleled.

Bartolozzi and Maioli is a workshop right out of the 14th century, where close to 40 artisans take orders from all over the world for statues, woodcarvings and gargoyles.

Santa Maria Novella

Visit the Church of Santa Maria Novella to sample the entire Renaissance in one place. During the Renaissance, science and art were intertwined and, with the help of mathematics, artists revolutionized space in painting. The flat, one-dimensional art of the Middle Ages gave way to a new discovery called perspective, the mathematical rendering of the focus on the human form.

Getting In

SMART TIP

Most Oltrarno artisans are happy to have visitors peer into their workshops and many have showrooms or shops attached where you can peruse and purchase. If you ring the bell outside the **Pitti Mosaics** showroom, you'll discover the Florentine art called Pietra Dura—inlaid pictures made from hard stones.

Santa Maria Novella's façade is typical of those of the Florentine mid-15th century. Simple, playful forms, squares and circles, and elegant green and white marble enliven the entryway to the church.

THE CHURCH OF SANTA MARIA NOVELLA OFFERS A PRIMER
IN HOW ART CHANGED DURING THE RENAISSANCE.

Once inside, you'll find a veritable treasure trove of art.

The *Polyptych*, an altarpiece in a side chapel, is representative of the art of the Middle Ages. The figures and space are flat and the faces stylized.

Compare that piece to a fresco in the nave, the *Trinity* by **Massacio**. Though painted just 70 years later, the figures in Massacio's work have bulk and the faces individuality. The painting introduced perspective for the first time.

Beat the Crowds

SMART TIP

The Uffizi houses some of the best art Florence has to offer. The best bet to beat the crowds is to visit the museum during evening hours. You can also book a visit in advance by telephone (055-23885) to avoid long lines.

The frescoes by Domenico Ghirlandaio in the main altar round out the Renaissance experience. Painted in 1485, the figures and faces have truly come to life. In fact, Lorenzo de Medici's uncle commissioned the work and the biblical scenes are peopled with his family.

Uffizi
www.uffizi.com

Over the years, Lorenzo de Medici and his family commissioned so much art that their palace overflowed with it. Eventually, they began to store their artwork here, in their administrative offices, and the Uffizi museum was born.

The first 15 rooms of the Uffizi are dedicated to the Florentine Renaissance.

The Madonna altarpieces in room two provide a primer in the development of Renaissance art. All three are by 13th-century artists but the *Madonna di Ognissanti* by **Giotto**, often considered one of the first painters of the Renaissance, is the most realistic of the three. The stylized, one-dimensional figures are on the brink of becoming fuller and more individual.

The portrayal of the individual may have reached its zenith in the work of **Leonardo da Vinci**. His unfinished *Adoration of the Magi* is strikingly modern. Brilliant and rich with ideas, Leonardo often left his work unfinished. He felt that his hands could never adequately express the perfection of his ideas.

All but ignored until the late 19th century, the **Sandro Botticelli** paintings housed in the Uffizi are now some of the most popular in the gallery. Botticelli and Lorenzo de Medici were close friends and the painter often took part in Lorenzo's roundtable discussions of Plato and the ancients. Consequently, secular themes and the legacy of ancient Greece are displayed prominently in Botticelli's work. He peopled his ideal world with his friends—Lorenzo, in particular. The model for Venus is thought to be Simonetta Vespucci, the mistress of Lorenzo's brother and a renowned Florentine beauty.

Not all Florentines embraced the new philosophies of the Renaissance. One man, a monk named Savonarola, preached at the Duomo to a crowd of 10,000 people, denouncing the pleasures of the senses and love of the arts. So passionate was he that Savonarola organized a "bonfire of the vanities" at the Piazza della Signora to burn frivolous items like hair ribbons, mirrors, wigs, Renaissance paintings and books. No one was immune. Many of Lorenzo de Medici's artist and philosopher friends repented and even Lorenzo—on his deathbed—asked pardon from Savonarola. Eventually Savonarola himself was burned at the stake. The deaths of Savonarola and Lorenzo brought an end to the golden age.

Side Trips

The Medici family owned several villas outside of town, and Lorenzo the Magnificent in particular loved to retreat to the country.

The **Villa Poggio a Caiano** was commissioned by young Lorenzo, who, in addition to his banking and statesman duties, fancied himself a poet and a scholar. It was at Medici villas that he and the most famous artists and thinkers of the Renaissance drank wine and engaged in philosophical debates. They called their group the Platonic Academy, for they loved discussing Greek philosophy, most particularly Plato. The portico on the villa resembles a Greek temple and the frescoes in the upstairs drawing room depict stories of the Medici family in the guise of Roman heroes.

Museum-less Art

SMART TIP

The churches of Florence house some of the city's best art and they are easier to access than museums.

> *Plato believed that an ideal form for everything exists in our memories—like an ideal garden. Before birth we witnessed these perfect forms in another world, and we spend our lives on earth trying to recollect what we saw. For the Renaissance artists this meant that man could find the ideal—divinity—within himself, a notion that was both frightening and exhilarating.*

The lovely medieval village of **Artimino** offers a great break from art and museums. Quiet streets, friendly locals and a cantina where you can buy the local wine make Artimino the perfect setting for a picnic lunch.

Several kilometers from Artimino lies the picturesque town of **Vinci**, home of Leonardo da Vinci. A painter, engineer, architect and scientist, Leonardo represents the quintessential Renaissance man. The town's Museo Leonardo da Vinci (**www.leonet.it**) is dedicated to his inventions. In his lifetime, Leonardo sketched designs for hundreds of inventions, and the museum has created many of them—from a perfectly modern bicycle to a mechanical car.

SMART DINING

Try the family-run *trattoria* **La Baruciola** (61 Via Maggio), where you can experiment with a little of everything. In Italy, a traditional meal has five courses: an appetizer, a *primo* (pasta or rice), a *secondo* (meat or fish), some *formaggio* (cheese) and then a *dolce* (dessert).

Vinesio (Borgo San Frediano 145), a restaurant in the Oltrarno, is trendy and reasonably priced with great food and wines.

Taverna del Bronzino (Via delle Ruote, 25r) happens to be located in a 15th-century Renaissance artist's studio.

For lively after-dinner entertainment, try the **Piazza San Spirito**, where bartenders dance the night away in the shadow of a church designed by Brunelleschi.

SMART LODGING

Once a 15th-century monastery, the **Villa San Michele**, designed by Michelangelo, is incredibly charming. Located a few minutes outside of Florence, the hotel has its own shuttle bus to make the trip to town. In the hot summer, nothing beats this cool, wooded retreat. You can check out the views of Florence from the pool or explore the nearby town of Fiesole (**www.fiesole.com**), which has its own Roman amphitheater. **www.villasanmichele.orient-express.com**

Rome

Tourism Web Site: www.enjoyrome.com

Tourist Office: Via Parigi 11
00185 Roma
Tel: 011-39-06-488-991
Fax: 011-39-06-481-9316

Rome is a living museum, where the ancient and modern live side by side. Here Caesar ruled, chariots raced, gladiators fought and Western civilization was born. In Rome, you can dine next to a temple to Jupiter, get your bearings on a Roman column or see ancient frescoes unearthed. Modern Rome is alive and well, however, and it swarms all around the ancient city.

If you pay a visit to the Termini train station in Rome, you'll find $170 million in recent improvements that don't alter the original 1920s architecture. The station now includes an indoor piazza with eateries and shops, an elevated restaurant, Rome's biggest bookshop and decorative orange trees. New electronic technology increases train capacity from 580 to 800 trains per day.

Via Sacra
The Via Sacra leads to the Roman Forum, the heart of early Rome. In ancient times, prominent citizens would visit the Forum each morning to discuss business and politics in the Curia, or Senate building. From the Rostrum, Mark Antony may have called out for his "friends, Romans and countrymen" to avenge the death of Julius Caesar.

Via Sacra was ancient Rome's busiest street. For hundreds of years, Roman legions swept across the Mediterranean, amassing an empire that stretched from Britain to North Africa to Persia. Following a battle, victorious generals, their cheeks painted red, rode down Via Sacra in their gilded chariots. Behind them, carts loaded with the spoils of war would follow along with paintings of the battle and a long procession of soldiers and prisoners.

Ancient civilizations honored their gods with rituals and sacrifice seeking good fortune, and Rome was no exception. Romans surrounded the Forum with temples to bring good luck to the city and its rulers. The **Temple of Vesta**, located here, housed the sacred fire of Rome and it was the job of the vestal virgins to keep it lit. Chosen when they were children, the vestal virgins vowed 30 years of chastity. If they strayed, they were buried alive.

The Palatine Hill

The Palatine Hill is just a short walk from the Forum and it offers a splendid view of the city below. A walk alone among the orange trees and cypress groves is a terrific way to escape the heat and crowds in the city's center.

Centuries ago, the Imperial Palace stood here. Now, the ruins of houses, courtyards and sunken stadiums are the only traces of the great wealth and luxury that Rome's elite enjoyed.

Colosseum

In its heyday, Rome offered its citizens plenty of food and fun to pacify them. The emperors hosted free games here in the Colosseum to entertain the general populace.

A typical day in the Colosseum started with a comic, bloodless battle between women or dwarfs. An early afternoon show featured the stalking and killing of hippos. Then, gladiators took to the ring, brandishing swords, pikes or red-hot bars. When a gladiator fell he could appeal to the crowd for mercy. A sea of waving cloth and upturned thumbs freed the man, but more often than not the crowd gave a thumbs-down.

ANCIENT ROME EXISTS SIDE BY SIDE WITH MODERN ROME. AFTER 2,000 YEARS, THE COLOSSEUM IS STILL A MAJOR TOURIST ATTRACTION, AND A GREAT EXAMPLE OF ROMAN ENGINEERING. TO THE LEFT IS THE ARCH OF CONSTANTINE.

Baths of Caracalla

In ancient Rome, unemployment was high and private dwellings were miserable, so most Romans spent their time in public, secular buildings. The Baths of Caracalla was such a place. Fed by the Roman aqueducts, another engineering marvel, the baths provided a place for Romans to soak in hot and cold pools, visit the gym, art gallery, library or snack bar. In its heyday, the complex was adorned with more gold, marble and artwork than any other building in Rome.

Fountains are the music of Rome. And some of them are still fed by Roman aqueducts. In ancient times, the fountains provided Rome's public water supply. Now they offer relief from the hot Roman sun.

Centro Storico

Start your tour of Rome's historic center in **Piazza della Rotunda**, where you'll find the **Pantheon**, a temple dedicated to the gods of the seven planets. The interior of the Pantheon is much the same today as when it was built in the second century A.D. by the emperor Hadrian. The hole in the ceiling of the Pantheon is a window to the heavens. Hadrian designed the ceiling so that the sun would sweep through the building like a spotlight.

At nearby **Campo dei Fiori**, the "field of flowers," you'll find a fruit and vegetable market every weekday morning. Just around the corner is Rome's finest Renaissance palace, the **Palazzo Farnese**. Also hidden away in these back streets is one of Rome's most charming fountains, **la Fontana delle Tartarughe**, the "turtle fountain." The turtles weren't part of the original 16th-century design. The artist Bernini added them later. Finish your walk at the breathtaking **Teatro di Marcello**, an ancient theatre that has been converted into an apartment building.

San Clemente

San Clemente offers visitors a glimpse of Rome's rich history layer by layer.

The façade of the church was built in the 18th century, but when you step inside you'll find yourself in a medieval church filled with glowing mosaics that are nearly 1,000 years old. These mosaics are some of the most unusual in Rome. The living cross grows from a vine and symbolizes salvation, while the doves symbolize the apostles and the drinking deer baptism.

When you've finished looking at the mosaics, head to the back of the church where a door takes you down to a fourth-century Christian church that was pillaged by Normans, buried and forgotten. The wall of the church features one of the first examples of written Italian.

SMART TIP

Bring a Map

Bring your own tourist map or written information when you visit Rome's ruins. They are not available at the sites themselves.

Watch for Pickpockets

When in Rome...pay attention! Pickpockets frequent the area around the Forum and Colosseum, as well as other areas of Rome, and they can spot a tourist a mile away.

ROME IS JUSTLY FAMOUS FOR ITS SPECTACULAR ART IN PUBLIC PLACES, SUCH AS THESE BAROQUE SCULPTURES AND FOUNTAINS IN PIAZZA NAVONA BY BERNINI. IN ANCIENT TIMES, PIAZZA NAVONA WAS A "CIRCUS" OR RACETRACK.

Take another set of stairs down and you'll find yourself in a second-century *mithraeum* where members of a mysterious cult sacrificed bulls to the Persian god Mithra.

Through the mithraeum you'll find an even older labyrinth of Roman streets, buildings, rivers and lakes.

St. Peter's, "Vatican City"
www.vatican.va

The bus is Rome's major form of public transportation (they could only put down two subway lines in the city because they kept digging up ancient ruins) and a great way to get to Vatican City. Buy your ticket in advance at a nearby tabacchi or tobacco shop. Tabacchi also sell postal stamps, or *francoboli*.

When you step off the bus, you'll be in another country—literally. Vatican City occupies 109 independent acres within the city of Rome and is the seat of the Roman Catholic Church. Like any other country, it has its own coins, stamps and postal system.

The **St. Peter's Basilica** draws thousands of pilgrims and tourists year-round. The church is dedicated to the apostle Peter, the first Bishop of Rome. All popes are his spiritual descendants.

The inside of the basilica is enormous,

Riding the Bus

SMART TIP

The bus stops are called *fermata*. On the signs, an arrow shows the direction the bus is headed, and the stop you are standing at is shown in a box. Enter where it says "Entrata," and validate your ticket in the orange machine.

ornate and dramatic, the very definition of Baroque. American writer Henry James wrote that entering the church "seems not so much a going in somewhere as a going out."

Fast Mail

SMART TIP

If you have a postcard or letter to mail, do it here. The Pope's mail is far more reliable than the Romans'.

Michelangelo designed St. Peter's famous dome, which has been copied by architects since. (Americans might recognize their own Capitol Dome in Washington, D.C.) Michelangelo also designed the uniforms worn by the Swiss guards in Vatican City. The guards were first hired to protect the Pope in the 16th century.

A good walk from Saint Peter's is the **Vatican Museum** (**www.christusrex.org/www1/ vaticano/o-Musei.html**), which contains one of the biggest and best collections of art in the world. The **Sistine Chapel** is the jewel of the museum. The ceiling is Michelangelo's vision of the Creation, original sin and the Flood. Flanking the Biblical scenes are portraits of prophets. At the center, God gives life to Adam in a scene that mirrors the artistic process.

Via del Corso

This long, boutique-lined street served as a racetrack in the 18th century. **Via Condotti**, which runs from the **Corso** to the **Piazza di Spagna**, is a veritable shopping mecca. When you've tired of shopping, take a seat on the **Spanish steps**, a great place to contemplate your purchases and people-watch. This area of Rome has attracted foreigners since the 19th century. In fact, the poet Keats lived in the Piazza for a time, right next to the steps.

Trastevere

For a more peaceful shopping experience, head to Trastevere, a neighborhood on Rome's left bank. One unique shop, **Polvere di Tempo** (Via del Moro, 59), sells, among other things, time. Owners Adrian Rodriguez and Mariana Nye handcraft almost all the items in this magical little shop.

Depending on when you visit, Rome can be hot. As you wander the city, take refuge from the heat in cool, dark churches. **Santa Maria in Trastevere**, one of the oldest churches in Rome, is a 12th-century church built over a 4th-century basilica. Some say this was the first place Christians were allowed to worship in public.

Take a Walk

SMART TIP

The area between the Pantheon, Piazza Farnese and the Teatro Marcello makes for a great walk. From the Pantheon, start wandering toward the river. As you wind your way through the streets of Centro Storico, you'll come upon **Piazza Navona** and its famous fountains that were designed by the 17th-century artist Bernini.

Nightlife

Rome comes alive at night, when you'll find the streets and piazzas pulsing. **Piazza Navona** and **Piazza di Spagna** are both hangouts for Romans. It's an Italian tradition to stroll around these piazzas after dinner and enjoy the sites. You may not have noticed them in the daylight, but there are cafés and beer gardens here that turn up the magic at night. **Trastevere** is another hot spot in the city.

SHAFTS OF LIGHT STREAM INTO THE INTERIOR OF THE PANTHEON, THE BEST-PRESERVED BUILDING FROM ANCIENT ROME. TO ANCIENT ROMANS, THE HOLE IN THE ROOF WAS "A WINDOW TO THE HEAVENS." SINCE THE SIXTH CENTURY, THE PANTHEON HAS BEEN A CHRISTIAN CHURCH.

SMART DINING

Best pizzerias in Rome:
For sit-down pizza, try the **Pizzeria Al Leoncino** (Via del Leoncino 28).

For pizza by the slice, try the **Pizzeria da Pasquale** (Via dei Prefetti 34/A).

To bring home a bottle of fine Italian wine, visit the **Enoteca al Parlamento** (Via dei Prefetti 15), which houses a great selection of Italian wines—and you don't have to be an expert to purchase. Describe the type of wine you like and the staff will assist you with a recommendation and a sample. U.S. residents can import two bottles of wine duty-free.

Reading

SMART TIP

If you're interested in learning more about ancient Rome, read *The Romans* by Kathryn Welch.

SMART LODGING

Hotel Listings: www.venere.it/roma

RUDY:
When in Rome, stay in a delightful convent called the **Istituto San Giuseppe** located on the Esquiline Hill near the Colosseum.

Situated between Santa Maria Maggiore and the "Cathedral of Rome and the World," San Giovanni in Laterano, the convent is near the Metro stations Manzoni and Vittorio Emanuele and only a short taxi ride from Stazione Termini, the main train station.

On the quiet Via Angelo Poliziano, a side street off the major tree-lined avenue, Via Merulana, the convent creates a walled island of tranquility in an otherwise bustling area of town. The sisters offer single, double and triple rooms, many of which are furnished with antiques; most have private baths (ask for one overlooking the elegant garden). There is a curfew—10:30 p.m. during the summer and 10 p.m. the rest of the year. The sisters speak several languages, including Italian, English, German, French, Portuguese and Spanish. This is a popular area, and the nuns recommend reserving a room three to four months in advance. The price is 70,000 lira (about U.S. $35) per person per night, including breakfast. Half- and full-board arrangements can be made and parking is available.

Bring Coins

SMART TIP

Bring some change for the coin-operated lights in Roman churches—the expense is well worth it.

■ ■ ■ ■   # Naples and the Amalfi Coast

Tourism Web Site: www.naplescity.com

Tourist Office: Piazza dei Martiri 58
80121 Napoli
Tel: 011-39-081-405-311
Fax: 011-39-081-401-961

Deep in the heart of Italy lies the birthplace of pizza, Caruso and Sophia Loren. This southern city, **Napoli**, is also home to some of the world's great historic treasures and only a stone's throw away from Europe's most spectacular drive.

Naples, a boisterous urban center, is the kind of city many of us picture when we think of a real Italian city. Smoldering in the shadow of Mt. Vesuvius, Naples is big, crowded and *molto Italiano*. This is a city full of extremes and, amid the chaos, you'll find some of the best historic sites of the ancient world.

Naples curves like a theater around its dazzling bay, but it's the city's streets that put on the show. One of the first things you'll notice about Neapolitans is their vitality and enthusiasm for life.

Like the volcano in the distance, Naples, Europe's most densely populated city, has a dramatic and slightly dangerous feel. Across frenetic streets, pedestrians dodge Vespas like ducks in a shooting gallery.

According to mythology, Naples was founded on the grave of a siren, one of the sea nymphs who sang out to sailors to lure them into wrecking their ships against the shore.

While the organized crime for which Naples is notorious still exists, it's not a problem for tourists. In Naples, your main concern should be pickpockets. In recent years, city leaders have worked hard to make the city safer, but caution is still advised.

Cappella Sansevero

The Cappella Sansevero, a fresco-and-marble extravaganza, is amazing for the sheer abundance of Baroque decoration. Elaborate and over-the-top, it was built as a burial place for a prominent Neapolitan family in the mid-18th century. The sculptures within

THE "VEILED CHRIST" BY SCULPTOR GIUSEPPE SAMMARTINO IS
THE CENTERPIECE OF CAPPELLA SANSEVERO, A BAROQUE EXPLOSION OF ART.
RUDY RATES CAPPELLA SANSEVERO AS "A CAN'T-MISS SITE" IN NAPLES.

Sansevero are as remarkable as the frescoed ceiling. Be sure to check out the alabaster image of Christ that seems to emerge from a transparent veil, and the figure draped with a fishing net carved from marble.

Duomo
The city's cathedral sits on a spot that's been occupied by religious buildings since ancient times and is dedicated to San Gennaro, Naples' patron saint. The Duomo is the site of a very mysterious Neapolitan ritual. In the chapel, under lock and key, are two vials of San Gennaro's dried blood. Three times a year, Neapolitans gather here to watch as the blood miraculously liquefies. Legend holds that if it doesn't liquefy, disaster will strike the city. Scientists are at a loss to explain the strange phenomenon.

Archaeological Museum
www.marketplace.it/museo.nazionale
Naples' National Archaeological Museum is considered to be one of the most important in the world. The collection contains works gathered from Pompeii and other cities that were devastated when Vesuvius erupted, as well as artifacts from the ancient city of Rome.

One of the most spectacular attractions at the museum is a mosaic that was lifted from the floor of the House of Faun at Pompeii. Measuring 19 feet by 10.5 feet, the mosaic shows Alexander the Great leading his cavalry against the fleeing Persian soldiers. The museum also boasts a fine collection of everyday items from Pompeii like spoons and mirrors.

Santa Chiara
In Naples' historic quarter, you'll find Santa Chiara, a Gothic church built in the early 14th century. It is within the walls of this church that you'll find several tombs of the

Angevins, the Frenchmen who ruled Naples for 200 years before being tossed out by the Spanish.

> *After Rome fell and the northern hordes overran the former empire, Europe spent many centuries reinventing itself. The Italian peninsula became a conglomeration of city-states, finally at the mercy of larger and more powerful northern nations. This country didn't actually become a single nation until well into the 19th century.*

The most spectacular part of Santa Chiara is outside in the *Cloisters of the Clares*. Take a stroll through the courtyard's wisteria-lined walkways and imagine a time when the painted *majolica* tiles were love letters to this small corner of tranquility.

Pompeii
www.touritaly.org/pompeii/pompeii-main.htm
Located just 15 miles outside Naples, Pompeii is a passport to ancient history.

To find the ruins, take the train that says "Pompeii/Scavi." If you take the train that says "Pompeii," you'll end up in the modern city of Pompeii.

On August 24, 79 A.D., the sky blackened, the air filled with poisonous clouds and terror struck the hearts of the city's 20,000 citizens. Mt. Vesuvius had erupted and Pompeii was buried under a mass of volcanic ash and mud. Men and women, children and animals, were stopped suddenly in their tracks. At the time, Pompeii was a busy commercial center and resort town. Now, it is an ancient city that has been frozen in time.

RUDY PONDERS A VICTIM OF THE 79 A.D. ERUPTION OF MT. VESUVIUS. THE VOLCANO EXPLODED, BURYING THE CITY OF POMPEII UNDER A CLOUD OF POISONOUS GAS AND TONS OF ASH. MANY VICTIMS—LIKE THIS MAN—WERE FOUND EERILY FROZEN IN TIME.

The vast ruins of Pompeii offer fascinating insights into the life of ancient Romans. It's as if their daily activities were preserved in a time capsule. The Forum was the city's central plaza.

One of the highlights of your visit will be the **House of Faun**, which is believed to have belonged to one of the wealthiest families in Pompeii. The house, which took up an entire city block, had four dining rooms—one for each season—and two gardens—one for winter and one for summer. The house is named for the whimsical statue of a faun found in one of its indoor ponds during excavation in the 19th century.

Buy a Gelato

SMART TIP

When purchasing a gelato in Italy, you pay for it first and then give your ticket to the person scooping.

Today, the volcano at Vesuvius is still active, having last erupted in 1944. Locals live in fear of the day the mountain will once again vent its wrath on the countryside.

Phlegraen Fields

Just west of Naples lie the Phlegraen Fields, or "fields of fire." This area, bursting with hot springs and sulfurous gases, floats freely on a mass of molten lava that is very close to the surface. In ancient times, people were both frightened and fascinated by the Phlegraen landscape. In fact, many believed the fields were the gateway to the underworld.

When Imperial Rome reached its prime in the first century, the Phlegraen fields became a fashionable spot for vacation villas. During their holidays, the Roman elite would visit posh spas here, taking in the views and soothing their weary bones. Today you can still try out these natural saunas, nicknamed "Purgatory" and "Hell."

Sorrento
www.itwg.com/ct_00160.asp

The town of Sorrento is just 30 miles from Naples and boasts a view of one of Italy's most stunning coastlines. The natural coves in and around Sorrento inspired dozens of 19th-century Romantic artists.

Sorrento is touristy, but that's OK. The town is clean and safe, and most of the store clerks speak English. If you love to shop, visit the old town, where pastel shops line the narrow stone streets and you'll find some of the best gelato on the coast.

Sorrento comes alive on holidays, when the town draws Italians and visitors alike. It's a great opportunity for people-watching and sampling **limoncello,** *a tart and dangerously enticing liqueur made with lemons plucked from the surrounding hillsides.*

Capri
www.caprionline.com

When you've finished with Sorrento, Capri makes an easy day trip. The ferry drops you at the island's busy Marina Grande, where you can catch the funicular to take you 500 feet up the hill to the town of Capri. In the summer, boats visit Capri constantly, emptying hordes of visitors onto the island. To avoid the stampede, visit Capri in the spring or fall.

Amalfi Coast
www.italiantourism.com

As enchanting as Capri is, it's only the beginning of southern Italy's natural wonders. The scenic Amalfi Coast, which runs 43 miles from Sorrento to Salerno, is dotted with sun-bleached towns that cling to craggy cliffs. As early as the ninth century, the Amalfi became an Italian maritime republic, rivaling Venice and other ports for dominance of the sea and inspiring some of the country's most astounding feats of civil engineering. Driving along the coast is not for the weak at heart. With its sheer cliffs and hairpin turns, the highway that runs along the Amalfi is among the most beautiful and most treacherous in the world. If you're not up for the white-knuckle driving, you can hop on a local bus to take in the awe-inspiring vistas. Check with the local tourist office for bus schedules and stops.

Paestum

Paestum, a two-hour drive from Sorrento, offers visitors a sample of some of the best Greek ruins outside of Greece. Six hundred years before Christ, Greeks colonized this spot, calling it the "City of Poseidon." It later fell to the Romans and then other invaders—all of whom were eventually driven out by mosquitoes. According to lore, swarms of the insects made this site very undesirable, and it sat abandoned for hundreds of years. In the 18th century, a crew of road builders stumbled across the ruins— three of the finest intact Greek temples in the world—in the middle of a forest.

THE CITY OF NAPLES CURVES GRACEFULLY AROUND THE BAY OF NAPLES IN
THE SHADOW OF MOUNT VESUVIUS, A STILL-ACTIVE VOLCANO.
NAPLES IS EUROPE'S MOST DENSELY POPULATED CITY.

The country roads leading out of Paestum offer a taste of the local specialty, Mozzarella di bufalo, a cheese made of buffalo milk. If you're a fan of the insalata caprese, a salad made with tomatoes, mozzarella di bufalo, olive oil and a dash of vinegar, you may have tasted this cheese in the United States.

Positano

Positano can be described simply as a cliffhanger of a town. The hills on which it is built are thrillingly steep and crowded with houses that seem to cascade down to the sea. Instead of streets, you navigate the town via a network of steep steps.

For a more ethereal perspective, take in the views Positano has to offer from several trails in the hills high above.

Penny-Pinchers Beware

SMART TIP

Penny-pinchers take heed; the prices in Positano—a popular destination of the rich and famous—are as steep as its hills.

SMART DINING

Caffe Gambrinus, Naples' oldest coffeehouse, was the "in place" for Neapolitan artists and intellectuals in the last century. The vaulted ceilings and frescoes still conjure images of Old World elegance. Treat yourself to one of the café's delicious pastries or a gelato. **www.gambrinus.it/caffe.htm**

Try pizza in its birthplace at one of the local pizzerias. The wood-fired pizza is to die for.

SMART LODGING

FROM RUDY MAXA'S TRAVELER NEWSLETTER

Get Thee to a Nunnery

"One does not come to Italy for niceness," claims Miss Lavish in E.M. Forster's *A Room With a View*. "One comes for life." And what a marvelous life it is! There is, however, a little-known element of Italy that is as mysterious as it is ordinary. One that can be found in a place, paradoxically, that is a step removed from the real world, yet an integral part of Italian culture. A place that is to be discovered in the convents and monasteries that grace the country's urban centers, rural landscapes and coastal villages.

Today, with dwindling numbers of novices and rising costs of maintaining their religious houses, many nuns and priests have opened their homes to the ecumenical public in an act of sheer brilliance. For budget and savvy travelers alike, this can mean paradise. For the last three years, Anne Walsh and her mother June have traveled through Europe researching religious sanctuaries that welcome guests for a book called *Bed and Blessings: Italy: A Guide to Convents and Monasteries Available for Overnight Lodging*. I asked Anne and June to pinpoint the very best places that visitors could stay in Italy's most sought-after cities and towns.

It's important to note that the people who greet you at monasteries and convents are religious men and women first, hoteliers second. They go about their daily life, attending early morning Mass, chanting and praying long before the sun has begun to rise. Today their faith and survival are intertwined, and as guests in their homes, you may benefit from an encounter as potentially intriguing as some of the monuments and museums you might explore during your visit.

Although Anne cautions that monastic rooms are normally Spartan, breakfast is plain and there is sometimes a curfew to which residents must adhere, staying in a religious guesthouse can offer very affordable accommodations in the heart of Italy's finest destinations.

On the fabled island of Capri, Anne discovered a fabulously situated convent called **Villa Helios**. A steep, narrow laneway wends its way up to the Villa's large blue gates where just beyond, a long, vine-covered canopy leads to a tiled foyer where visitors are greeted warmly. Many of the simply furnished rooms offer spectacular views of the sea. A profusion of tropical trees and flowers fill a garden that overlooks the island and the Bay of Naples. From the Villa, it's just a few minutes' walk into the charming town and its center, the **Piazza Umberto**. Villa Helios is open from Easter to October and has single, double and triple rooms, all with private baths. English is spoken, and the curfew is flexible. But guests who intend to return quite late should make arrangements beforehand with the staff.

To learn more about Villa Helios and make reservation inquiries, visit **www.villahelios.it**.

Hotel Minerva
One of my personal favorites. Located at Via Capo 30, Hotel Minerva offers visitors to Sorrento views of the Mediterranean and a cliff-hanging swimming pool. Tel: 081-878-1011

Phoning Home From Abroad

By Rudy Maxa

YES, NOW YOU CAN CARRY A CELL PHONE THAT WORKS in the United States and overseas.

Keeping in touch while abroad has always been difficult and expensive. Even brief calls from your hotel can be very costly. Pay phones—if you can figure out how to work them—gobble coins and work differently in different countries. But now a new line of wireless phones called dual-band phones has changed all that. These phones can cross borders seamlessly and have made calling home both easier and more affordable—although the initial cost can be as much as $600.

Top-of-the-line, dual-band phones are not the only option for staying in touch, however. If your budget is more limited, or if you don't travel abroad that often, you might consider buying or renting a phone for use overseas. Rental rates vary, but as a rule of thumb, if you plan to be away for two weeks or more, or expect to travel in the future, you're better off buying rather than renting a phone. But before you purchase, make sure you know what you're getting.

Phones that work everywhere

The world's digital phone networks operate under different systems, which is why most U.S. cell phones don't work overseas. In the early '90s, Europe and some parts of Asia adopted a common digital standard called Global System for Mobile Communications (GSM). In contrast, the U.S. digital network is carved up among several competing standards and is so fragmented that a phone that works in one part of the country might not work in another. (Although most digital phones these days get around this by defaulting to analog when out of their digital coverage area.)

Phones that work everywhere are called dual-band phones, which means they operate on both the frequency used for digital phones in the United States (1900 MHz) and the frequencies used by much of the rest of the world (900 or 1800 MHz). These phones are usually more expensive than your average cell phone. Nokia, Ericsson and Motorola make dual-band phones; prices vary from $200 to $600.

Before buying, remember that different phones work with different networks. Make sure the phone you pick has network coverage in areas you want. Then make sure you'll pay less per minute than you would by using one of the popular services such as those from AT&T or Sprint that let you call a toll-free number abroad and charge the call to your U.S.-based phone. Usually, it's no contest—the cell phone wins on a cost-per-minute basis. But if you only plan to make a handful of calls from overseas, why invest in a phone? One advantage: You can receive calls anywhere while traveling.

Buying a GSM phone

If you already own a U.S.-based cell phone and don't want to switch, consider buying a cheaper GSM phone to use when you travel. You can purchase a GSM phone at your destination or you can pick one up before you leave. I checked with two companies, WorldCell (at **www.worldcell.com**, referred to me by Nokia), and Ustronics (at **www.ustronics.com**, referred to me by Motorola). WorldCell's least expensive phone, (not including a used Nokia 2110 at $199), is a Nokia 3210 costing $295—not much cheaper than buying a dual-band phone you can use both in the United States and abroad. Ustronics prices are more reasonable: GSM-only phones start at less than $100.

Having a phone, of course, does you no good without a carrier to issue you a number and provide cell service. WorldCell offers service packages, Ustronics doesn't. But at $59 a month, WorldCell's service charges are steep. Before you purchase any plan, make sure you compare local and international rates, fees for incoming calls and connection fees.

If you buy a phone without a service package, you'll have difficulty obtaining service overseas unless you can prove you're a resident. You'll have to show a utility bill as well as provide a check from an account open at a local bank. In Europe, however, you get around this by buying a SIM card, and simply inserting it into your phone. The SIM card works like a prepaid calling card and comes with a phone number, and, depending on the company, an answering service, call waiting, instant messaging and call forwarding. When your initial minutes run out, you can refill the card without changing the phone number by dialing a number you buy that allows you to "download" another boatload of calling minutes. The initial kit, with the phone number and some start-up minutes, costs around $50, depending on the country. Refills are about $20.

Using a prepaid card can be a little bit more expensive, but then you only pay for the calls you make, and there's no monthly fee that a service contract entails. Prime-time calls (weekdays, 7 a.m.–7 p.m.) run between 50 cents and a dollar a minute, depending on the company and the country, and nights and weekends are usually half the prime-time rate. SIM cards (initial kits and refills) are sold on the Internet, in electronics shops, in supermarkets and at newsstands across Europe.

Renting a phone

If you're making a short trip and don't plan much overseas travel in the near future, renting a phone is probably the best option. WorldCell charges $75 for the first week and $50 per full week thereafter. Per-minute rates vary, depending on the country. The local rate for France, for example, is $2.06 per minute and calling back to the United States is $2.76 per minute.

As a comparison, my newsletter staff currently carries Motorola i2000 dual-band phones abroad. Price to buy the phone: $100 (at **www.nextel.com**). A monthly service fee of about $40 a month gives you a basket of minutes that can be used in the United States. Placing or receiving calls in most European countries costs $1 a minute; any fraction of a minute is rounded up to the next full minute. In Delhi, India, however, that rate triples to $3 a minute.

The bottom line: Owning a phone brings down your per-minute costs overseas. But if you just need a cell phone for a short period of time, why buy?

You can also rent phones that work overseas from travel agents, rental car companies, hotels or even credit card companies. WorldCell has special deals for Avis customers. The British Hotel Reservation Centre's (**www.bhrc.co.uk**) phone rentals start at a little more than $4 a day, plus phone call charges. American Express Platinum members can rent phones, including voice mail service, starting at $6 per day, plus phone call charges, from Rent-A-Phone (888-309-8560).

Want a satellite phone that should work anywhere around the globe? Visit **www.globalstar.com**.

Until the next big technological advance, when networks around the world work together, you'll have to assess your needs before deciding whether to rent or buy a phone. It's easier than ever to stay in touch while traveling abroad, but the options can be puzzling. And one thing is for sure: Two years from now, all the rules will be different.

Stay Connected

U.S. cell phones that will work abroad (All prices from **www.cellmania.com**)

Ericsson:

I888 WORLD for GSM 900 / GSM 1900MHz; $199
T28 for GSM 900 / GSM 1900MHz; $299
www.ericsson.com

Nokia:

Nokia 8890 for GSM 900 / GSM 1900MHz; $553
www.nokiausa.com

Motorola:

Timeport P7389 for GSM 900 / 1800 / 1900 MHz; $499
Timeport L7089 for GSM 900 / 1800 / 1900 MHz; $399
www.motorola.com

Medical Emergencies Abroad:
Don't Leave Home Until You Read This!

By Rudy Maxa

Last winter, while playing touch football, my newsletter contributing writer Brooke Comer fell on a sharp rock that lacerated her knee. Clearly, she needed stitches. What was not clear was where she would get them, because Brooke was in Cairo, Egypt. On the advice of a local friend, she took a cab to Kasr Al Alene Hospital, assured that this medical facility was on a par with America's finest.

But her friend neglected to tell her that there are two Kasr Al Alenes: a dilapidated public hospital, and a deluxe, private one. Brooke arrived at the former, where a stark lobby was littered with broken gurneys and veiled women shrieked against flyspecked walls. Three of the 20 patients waiting to be treated were bleeding profusely on the floor. Brooke limped out, returned to her hotel, and called the American embassy.

An embassy nurse gave her directions to the Shalaan Surgical Center, a private clinic owned by Dr. Karim Shalaan, an Egyptian surgeon with Ivy League degrees and an American accent. Brooke received seven stitches in a state-of-the-art operating room luxuriously appointed with marble floors and gold-leaf trim. She paid the $260 fee with a MasterCard, and her insurance later covered the full amount.

Brooke was lucky. Not everyone is able to reach an embassy nurse. Not everyone has access to a good clinic.

Even when hospitals are within easy reach, you may fare better at a clinic. Dr. John Padilla, a plastic surgeon practicing in Santa Barbara, California, who has worked extensively in South America, advises travelers to choose private clinics over hospitals. "If you need medical attention in Latin America, don't ask to be taken to a hospital," he says. "Ask for a *clinica*. That's where you'll find the best-quality care." Clinicas are usually small, private medical facilities owned by American-educated doctors who cater to wealthy locals and may offer a higher standard of technology and hygiene than city hospitals.

You can find U.S. embassy–approved clinics and specialists in the country you're going to visit by checking that embassy's web site and requesting a consular information sheet.

Even when you do find medical care abroad, the cost of treatment or medical evacuation to a U.S. hospital can be as frightening as what ails you. I recommend purchasing medical evacuation insurance, especially if you rely on Medicare, which does not provide coverage for hospitals or doctors outside the United States. Medical airlifts can cost $20,000 to $50,000. Virtually all travel insurance policies also include helpful hotlines, so members can locate English-speaking doctors and clinics anywhere.

International SOS Assistance sells a $280 Global Assistance Plan that covers all costs of medical evacuation for trips up to 120 days in one year. For shorter trips, medical evacuation insurance costs $55 (14 days) and $98 (30 days) per person. But you can't request to be flown to your hometown hospital; company doctors make that judgment call. You can add medical coverage up to $10,000 for $35 a month, good for up to 180 days.

Travel Assistance International, under the Worldwide Assistance umbrella, is a good buy for large families. Medical evacuation, covered 100 percent, costs $88 per person, or $188 per family regardless of size (as long as all children are dependents) for up to 92 travel days per year. But again, Worldwide Assistance, not the member, decides which medical facility best suits the patient's needs. You can also buy evacuation and medical insurance (up to $15,000) in one package for $75 per person or $115 per family, for trips up to 14 days.

Medjet Assistance costs $150 a year or $225 for a family of five, and evacuations are fully covered. Members, regardless of medical necessity, are airlifted in planes configured specifically for medical missions. Thus patients are not delayed while the need for evacuation is approved by company doctors. A major advantage of Medjet: Members—not insurance company doctors—choose which medical facility to go to. If you require hospitalization, Medjet will fly you from a distant point to your hometown hospital, if that's your wish.

Membership does have its privileges, and privilege has its price; American Express Platinum cardholders pay a $300 annual fee, which entitles them to medical evacuation coverage from any country (but not to any hospital—the provider makes that choice). Green and Gold AmEx cardholders, who pay annual fees of only $50 and $75, don't get evacuations, but they do get access to the company's free, 24-hour Global Travel Assistance Hotline, which locates approved, English-speaking clinics and specialists worldwide.

IAMAT, International Association for Medical Assistance to Travelers, does not provide medical evacuation, but does offer a global network of doctors to assist travelers abroad. Membership in the nonprofit organization is free, and members receive a directory listing phone numbers, street and e-mail addresses of doctors around the world, plus pamphlets about other health-related travel issues. IAMAT identifies centers in each city outside the United States that can set up appointments for travelers with appropriate specialists. Members are responsible for the fees that range from $55 to $95.

Hopefully, you'll never find yourself in Brooke's predicament. But if you do, it's better to be prepared than to rely on luck or the kindness of strangers when it comes to medical treatment.

Just the Facts

- U.S. State Department's Medical Information for Americans Traveling Abroad, a list of companies that provide medical evacuation services, travel assistance and insurance, is available at **www.travel.state.gov/medical.html**. To receive Consular Information Sheets that describe the state of health care in a country, go to **www.travel.state.gov** or call from the telephone on your fax to have the info faxed to you: 202-647-3000.

- For detailed information on physicians abroad, check at your public library for The Office ABMS (American Board of Medical Specialists), a directory of Board Certified Medical Specialists.

- Health Information for International Travel, a 210-page government book, can be ordered by mail from the Superintendent of Documents, P.O. Box 371954, Pittsburgh, PA, 15250, or by calling 202-512-1800.
Request publication #017-023-00202-3. Cost: $22.

- International SOS Assistance: 800-523-8930.

- MEDJET: 1-800-9MEDJET or **www.medjet.com**

- Worldwide Assistance/Travel Assistance International: 800-821-2828 (8 a.m.–5 p.m. Central Standard Time); or **www.worldwideassistance.com**

- IAMAT: 716-754-4883 (8 a.m–4 p.m. Eastern Standard Time); or **www.sentex.net/~iamat**; e-mail: **iamat@sentex.net**

- American Express: 800-368-6924 or **www.americanexpress.com**

- U.S. State Department's Overseas Citizens Service: **202-647-5225**. Give this number to friends and relatives at home; if there is an emergency abroad, this is the 24-hour number they may call for info.

Mi Casa, Su Casa:
Swapping Homes with a Stranger Overseas—Would You Dare?

By Rudy Maxa

Have you ever thought of trading lives with someone overseas? There are a number of companies that help facilitate international house-swapping. And while you can't exactly live someone else's life, you can at least sample it by staying in their home, driving their car, shopping where they do, and greeting their neighbors.

My friend Gary Wasserman, a Washington-based political consultant, and his wife, Ann, a high school biology teacher, decided they wanted to swap their downtown D.C. home and take a summer vacation overseas with their teenage daughter. They figured since their house would be empty and their car unused while they traveled, they weren't giving up anything. And getting a free house instead of paying for lodging abroad would allow them to stay longer for a lot less money.

Making things easier was Intervac, a San Francisco–based company that publishes a catalogue five times a year offering 5,000 houses available for exchange in dozens of countries. For less than $100, the Wassermans listed their house with a photograph and a description.

"Like most simple ideas," Gary told me afterwards, "this one became more complicated the closer we got to it. House-exchanging requires both fastidious organization and considerable flexibility, a combination of virtues not evenly distributed among families, including mine."

The Wassermans' experience holds lessons for anyone who's ever thought about trading places for a vacation.

The Beginning

First of all, Intervac said that great homes tended to be claimed quickly. So the Wassermans had to decide in September of the year before they wanted to travel where they wanted to vacation. They needed to list their preference in their ad that would appear in the December catalogue.

They knew they wanted to be in France, since their son was spending his junior year in college in Paris. But "the science of predicting a 21-year-old's whereabouts a year in advance hasn't gotten very far," Gary told me. By the time he'd homed in on a place near Paris, his son decided he wouldn't be staying in the city after his spring semester. The Wassermans turned down an offer of a home from a family in Grenoble because "there were six of them wanting to stay longer at our place than we wished to stay at theirs."

But a fax from a couple with a teenager in Montpellier, near the Mediterranean, along the Cote d'Azur, caught the Wassermans' interest. They liked the picture in the catalogue, both families were willing to travel on the same dates, and so a match was made.

Except when the Wassermans arrived in Montpellier, the cab driver didn't drop them off in front of the handsome, two-story house whose picture they'd admired in the Intervac catalogue. Instead, they found themselves with a small, two-bedroom apartment "in a commercial area which had a number of unattached men drinking wine on the corner with their large dogs." The car the family left for them was an old Nissan diesel with 100,000 miles on the odometer, a flat front tire, and no jack in the trunk. The windows, lacking screens, invited mosquitoes; the flat had no air-conditioning. And about every 20 minutes, trains passed near their bedroom window, day and night.

"On several hot nights," Gary told me, "my wife and I would lie in bed awaiting the trains and breaking the reverie with thoughts of what was happening to our D.C. home. She, a resolute nonsmoker, fantasized about the all-night, bring-your-own-Gaulois parties our French guests were having. Then we'd argue about whose idea this had been in the first place."

It wasn't until the Wassermans returned to Washington and took another look at the Intervac catalogue that they learned they'd made a mistake. The catalogue's description of the Montpellier apartment was under a picture that went with the description above. "We felt dumb," Gary admits.

The Reality

In fact, though, the Wassermans soon began to fit into their new life. Outside of town, they had their choice of mountains or beaches. A two-hour drive to the east took them to the lovely nature preserve of Camargue, where the family spent two days hiking around lagoons, watching flamingos and other wildlife. They ended both days with dinner in the beach town of Les Saintes-Maries-de-la-Mer, which had a bullfighting ring and cafes that served paella.

The most pleasant beach was at Palavas, a half-hour's drive from their apartment. The town featured a Ferris wheel and a canal lined with inexpensive restaurants. Palavas may have been situated along the French Riviera, but the region where the Wassermans vacationed was favored less by the jet set than by French city dwellers on summer vacations.

The family explored Romanesque churches in the small towns that dot the hills overlooking the coastline. Their favorite was in the village of St.-Guilhem-le-Desert, where they admired a church whose former interior decorations can be found as far afield as the Cloisters in Washington Heights, in New York City. Nearby rapids led to a lake that was perfect for afternoon swimming.

The Wassermans grew addicted to the duck served at Le Vieil Ecu, a restaurant very near their apartment, where the waiters were delighted to meet an American family. They got to know the workers at the all-night pâtisserie just down the street where they had croissants and café au lait every morning. They appreciated the ripe fruits and vegetables available in the local market. And Gary pronounced Montpellierites "about a zillion times friendlier" than Parisians.

Lessons Learned

In fact, after an inauspicious beginning, the Wassermans found themselves reluctant to leave after their two-week vacation. They arrived home to find their house much as they'd left it, with the addition of a bottle of good red wine and a courteous thank-you note.

"Neither the most paranoid nor the most pleasant of our expectations was fulfilled," Gary says today. "Would we do it again? Not right away. But soon, with more preparation next time."

I asked Gary to offer some advice to anyone interested in swapping homes. Here's what he had to say:

- Reduce expectations. Forget that chateau in the bucolic countryside, advises Gary. In all likelihood, the people with whom you're exchanging homes will get the larger, more modern residence.

- Get references. Many families trading houses have done it before. Ask for the names of Americans they've worked with. Then call them.

- Decide exactly what you want. It's easy to let offers arrive, but it's better to figure out where you want to be and why and then concentrate your energies on finding a home that matches your desires.

- Be flexible. That's slightly contradictory to the preceding bit of advice, but knowing where and what you want may still require accepting some second choices.

- Recruit a neighbor to help your guests. Your visitors will probably arrive knowing little about your home and surroundings. Having a neighbor greet them and provide them with some basic information is considerate, and it may help your peace of mind as well.

Details: Swap Shops

- HomeLink, 800-638-3841; **www.swapnow.com**; $35 to list your house

- House Swap U.S.A/Europe, 508 885-5264; **www.ultranet.com/~swap**; one-time fee of $25 to list your house

- Home Exchange.com, 805-898-9660; **www.homeexchange.com**; one-time fee of $30 to list your house

- International Home Exchange Network, 407-862-7211; **www.ihen.com**; membership is $29.95 per year

- Intervac U.S., 800-756-HOME; **www.intervac.org**; membership cost varies from country to country

- The Invented City, 800 788-2489; **www.invented-city.com**; $75 for a year's membership

- Teacher Swap, 516-244-284

- Trading Homes International, 800-877-8723; **www.trading-homes.com**; $65 per year to access e-mail addresses of members, but you can view the listings for free.

Smart Sites

Finding a Cyber Café in Europe
www.kiosek.com/eurocybercafes
www.cybercafe.com

These are two of the most reliable web sites on the subject. The first site boasts more than 1,000 listings in 40 European countries and the second lists about 3,000 cyber cafés around the world. Leave your laptop at home unless you want the convenience of accessing the Internet 24/7. If you can stand the separation, read e-mail and surf the Web at a cyber café. How to find one? Check with the locals, preferably students, or the program board at an American university abroad. No luck? Let your fingers do the walking through the local Yellow Pages. In the end, if you opt to take your computer, make certain it can safely run on 220 voltage. If not, remember to bring along a converter.

Changing Currency
www.swapcash.com

This site enables you to compare exchange rates among 16 online currency sellers and allows you to buy cash online and have it delivered right to your doorstep. Where to best exchange money is one of the age-old travel questions. Bottom line: Get your foreign currency through an ATM machine abroad. If you need some walking-around cash before your arrival, go ahead and pay your bank the five percent. Charges for buying or selling currency fluctuate madly all over the world. There is no "one" right way to do it for every country. Some exchange offices say they charge no fee or commission. In which case, they just offer less favorable exchange rates. Using your ATM card allows you to access currency at favorable bank wholesale rates. You'll probably be charged a bank fee every time you access your account—perhaps $1.50—so take out what you need for a few days; don't withdraw in $20 increments!

The Boom Chicago Comedy Show
www.boomchicago.nl

If you're planning a trip to Amsterdam, be sure to reserve an evening for the Boom Chicago Comedy Show. Nearly a decade ago, a group of students (all graduates of Evanston High School in Chicago), went on a post-college tour of Europe and ended up buying and renovating an old theater on Leidseplain Square. Now their dinner theater show is one of the city's most popular performances and tourist attractions. The cast of 12 rotates three English-language shticks in the style of *Saturday Night Live* (at its best) or Second City seven nights a week and has been selling out for seven years. Ticket prices are reasonable. For times and availability, call 011-020-423-0101 or visit the web site.

www.thinkparis.com

Brigitte Bardot has nothing on this ultra-romantic web site that reveals the best places to share a kiss in Paris. Recipes for love include smooching on a bench near the Café Bizarre, where rue des Vignoles meets rue Michel-de-Bourges, near the Buzenval metro stop, in the 20th arrondissement.

www.operabase.com

Go to this web site and click on search tools. Every production in town won't be listed. However, you can call your hotel ahead of time and ask the concierge to book tickets for you. Or check out posters around town after you arrive to find out about less well-known but often equally good performances by smaller companies.

Biographies

RUDY MAXA
HOST OF *SMART TRAVELS*, THE PUBLIC TELEVISION SERIES

Rudy Maxa is one of America's best-known travel writers—on radio, television, in cyberspace and in print. He's been a journalist for more than 20 years. His radio travel series *The Savvy Traveler*® quickly became the fastest-selling new show in the history of public radio and now airs on 180 stations across the country. The weekly hour radio program grew out of Rudy's years as travel commentator on public radio's nightly *Marketplace*.

Rudy Maxa writes on how to travel smart for *Worth*, the personal finance monthly, and contributes humorous travel essays to *Forbes* magazine. His *Maxa Miles* on business travel is a weekly column for MSNBC.com, and he appears as a travel expert on CNN, CNNfn, and Fox News Channel. *Rudy Maxa's Traveler*, a subscription-only newsletter, gives insider information on "traveling in style for less." He was a travel columnist with *American Express Online*, and wrote a monthly business travel column for the Dow Jones tabloid, *BIZ*.

As a *Washington Post* investigative reporter and personalities columnist, Maxa's reporting on political scandals was nominated by the paper for THE PULITZER PRIZE. During his tenure at *The Post*, he won the JOHN HANCOCK AWARD FOR EXCELLENCE in Business and Financial Journalism.

Rudy Maxa has written for an ABC-TV dramatic series and is an occasional guest travel authority on *The Today Show* and *Good Morning America*. His travel articles appear in *GQ*, *The Washington Post*, the *Los Angeles Times*, *USAirways Magazine*, *Playboy*, *Ladies Home Journal*, the *London Evening Standard*, *Modern Maturity*, *P.O.V.* and other magazines.

In addition to his lectures on travel, Rudy speaks frequently on politics and journalism. He spends half his time traveling. He calls Washington, D.C., home and has two children.

SMART TRAVELS
PRODUCTION TEAM

For 18 years, SMALL WORLD PRODUCTIONS has produced substantial, content-driven travel series for public television. The Seattle-based company has produced 91 half-hour episodes and two pledge specials that are popular with public television programmers and viewers. This body of work translates into more than a hundred home video titles. SWP production credits include *Smart Travels—Europe with Rudy Maxa*, *Travels in Europe with Rick Steves: Series I, II, III* and *IV, Travels in Mexico and the Caribbean with Shari Belafonte, America's Historic Trails with Tom Bodett, Best Travels in Europe* and *Best of the Mediterranean*. SWP programs have helped to raise tens of millions of dollars in viewer contributions to public television stations. SMALL WORLD's awards include CINE GOLDEN EAGLES, national TELLY AWARDS and a COLUMBUS INTERNATIONAL FILM FESTIVAL AWARD.

SWP partners Patricia Larson, Sandra Nisbet and John Givens created the series *Smart Travels—Europe with Rudy Maxa*. In addition to their body of work with SWP, Larson and Nisbet have a background in theater, history, play writing, international travel and teaching college. CEO Givens has been producing, directing and editing public television programs for more than 35 years. Programs produced and/or directed by Givens have won several EMMYS. He's a former member of the Board of Governors of the National Academy of Television Arts and Sciences, Seattle Chapter.

Larson and Nisbet teamed with Givens in 1980 to make public television programs supported by the National Endowment for the Humanities, the Washington Commission for the Humanities and the Washington State Arts Commission. Their credits include a dramatic series, *Take It To The People*, hosted by Stanley Kramer, and an award-winning documentary, *Everything Change, Everything Change*.

For this project, SMALL WORLD was joined by its team of award-winning photographers, editors and producer/writers. Producer Patty Conroy has won several TELLY AWARDS and two CINE GOLDEN EAGLES for her work with Small World, the Boeing Company and the University of Washington. Producer Susan McNally is currently writing and directing a feature-length comedy funded by the National Endowment for the Arts. Award-winning photographer Tom Speer, chief photographer at KCTS/Seattle, has shot more than 60 travel episodes for Small World. His other national credits include *Miracle Planet, Fire on the Rim, Death: The Trip of a Lifetime, Bill Nye the Science Guy, The Frugal Gourmet* and *The NewsHour*. Editor David Ris brings unique skills and knowledge of high-definition television production to the project. He has edited more than 24 travel episodes for SWP and does freelance work with the University of Washington and other clients. *Rudy Maxa's Smart Travels in Europe*, this companion book, was compiled with care from the research, writing and expertise of our host Rudy Maxa, our television producers, and editor Laura Mancuso. Mancuso, a founder and partner in MMMEDIA, a recruiting firm for broadcasting and news media. An experienced researcher, book editor and freelance writer, Laura works in San Francisco.

Acknowledgments

PRODUCING A TELEVISION SERIES AND WRITING A COMPANION BOOK are major undertakings that cannot be accomplished without prodigious help from scores of "accomplices." Acknowledging their help is gratifying. The main fear—shared by the producers and the book editors alike—is inadvertently leaving someone out. We begin with an apology to anyone who helped but is not listed below.

First, we want to thank our corporate sponsor, AMERICAN AIRLINES, for its support of the series. Special kudos to Tim Doke of American Airlines for believing in the project and for bringing it to the attention of his colleagues at the AA corporate headquarters in Dallas. And special thanks to EXPEDIA.COM for joining *Smart Travels* as a corporate underwriter. We are especially grateful to Richard Bangs and the corporate staff of Expedia for their kind financial support. EXPEDIA.COM—DON'T JUST TRAVEL, TRAVEL RIGHT.

The national tourist offices of many of the countries we visit have generously provided advice, support and contact information. They deserve special recognition here. Below is information on the many regional and local tourist offices that helped with the project as well. We particularly want to thank: Dottore Franco Ferrara and his fine staff at the ITALIAN GOVERNMENT TOURIST BOARD office in Los Angeles; Lilian Opsomer, BELGIAN TOUR-IST OFFICE; NETHERLANDS BOARD OF TOURISM; Lillian Hess, DANISH TOURIST BOARD; and the BRITISH TOURIST AUTHORITY. Stephanie Levin served as a liaison with local authorities, museums and businesses in Paris.

Special thanks are in order for several hotels featured in the series, including: ORIENT EXPRESS HOTELS in Venice, Florence and Portofino. We are pleased to feature the CIPRIANI in Venice, the SPLENDIDO in Portofino, and the VILLA SAN MICHELE in Florence in the book and in the television series. Certainly special thanks are in order for Patricia Harper of Orient Express Hotels' New York office for her help in gaining access to each of these splendid hotels. In London, we featured the ATHENAEUM HOTEL and learned about British afternoon tea from Sally Bulloch, the general manager of the hotel. Sally and the Athenaeum rate "two thumbs up" from Rudy and our crew—our highest rating.

Rental cars for **Smart Travels** were provided by AVIS INTERNATIONAL. Special thanks to Avis and Tom Kennedy of the company's U.S. office, for the clean, comfortable, reliable transportation. And kudos to Mariana Field Hoppin of MFH TRAVEL MARKETING, LTD., of New York, for all her help in arranging for Avis' kind support.

AMERICAN PUBLIC TELEVISION of Boston distributes the series nationally to public television stations. We especially appreciate the advice, direction and reviews of Nelsa Gidney who served as Executive Producer on the project for APT. And special thanks to Joe Zesbaugh, Chris Funkhouser and Kathryn Larsen of APT for their guidance, encouragement and commitment to the series.

KCTS, THE PUBLIC TELEVISION STATION IN SEATTLE, is a co-production partner. We couldn't have done the series without them. Tom Speer's photography is stunning, Lisa Moore and Rodney Shelden Fehsenfeld's graphic design is superb, and KCTS production manager Nolan Lehman has been accommodating and helpful. Kathy Mack deserves special recognition for her support and management of the project for KCTS.

Our heartfelt thanks to Timothy J. Lorang, production manager at the UNIVERSITY OF WASHINGTON'S VIDEO PRODUCTION UNIT where the series was edited in HDTV. Through Tim's leadership, the University of Washington became a co-production partner as well. Much of the technical expertise needed to succeed in producing the series was provided by Jerry Morin of UW Video Productions. His coaching, coaxing and cajoling guided us through the technical mazes of producing the series in HDTV and converting it to NTSC formats for broadcast over conventional television. Thank you, Jerry. And very special thanks to David Fulton for access to his amazing equipment.

As with all of our previous series and—we hope—our future series, the original music for *Smart Travels* was provided by Denny Gore at SAFARI STUDIOS and his talented cadre of musicians including Tom Hopkins, Mike Stoican, Denny Hall, Ted Turner, Joann Gillis and Han Teuber among others. They make us "sound good," and we appreciate that.

In several cities, we were the beneficiaries of kindness from local friends who went out of their way to show us their favorite places. In Paris and Rome, Daisuke Utagawa, chef and owner of Washington's premier Japanese restaurant, SUSHIKO, helped introduce us to the regional cuisine. He also cheerfully toted camera equipment, as did John Mitchell, a Washington editor of *Reader's Digest*, who built a Paris trip around our shooting. Also in Paris, Catherine Sullivan kindly opened her home to Rudy. In Genoa and the Italian Riviera, Dr. Roberto Stubinski and Dr. Maria Pia zipped around on a motorcycle to find and lead us to great locations for shooting. They also provided on-the-spot translation services.

At times, Rudy crisscrossed the Atlantic four times a week in order to be on location in Europe and still host his public radio show, *Savvy Traveler*®, in the United States. For budget reasons, most of those flights were in coach class. But on several occasions when space was available, Beth Perdue at LUFTHANSA, Jacqueline Pash at SABENA, Lotti Mara at ALITALIA, Honor Verrier at BRITISH AIRWAYS, and Tim Doke at AMERICAN AIRLINES secured

Rudy a seat in business class; a thirsty man in a desert couldn't have been more grateful. It was Courtney Froemming's idea to ask, and Rudy says, "Brilliant idea, Courtney." Rudy would also like to thank the *Savvy Traveler*® staff in Los Angeles including Jim Russell, J.J. Yore, Walter Cabral, Michelle Kholos, Ben Adair, Jim Gates, and Derry London for juggling radio taping schedules to accommodate his overseas work. On several occasions, they also worked double duty in order to complete two shows in a week so Rudy could spend an extended period working on the ground in Europe.

In Rudy's Washington office, Kim Lee, Heidi Daniel, Philip Chalk and William Harrison kept the trains running on time with the newsletter and other projects while Rudy was on the road. The staff at WAMU radio in Rudy's hometown of Washington, D.C., also accommodated his erratic radio show taping schedule, and thanks are due the engineers and management for their flexibility.

And, finally, Rudy thanks Lesley Trevillian, Alexander Maxa, and Kathy Frank for enduring his unusual absences during the 2000 shooting season. Each, for his or her own reasons, was inconvenienced by his schedule but accepted it in good cheer. The family members and loved ones of the entire on-the-road staff, in fact, tolerated lengthy absences and deserve a standing ovation for their understanding and support. We hope the finished product is a small recompense for the days spent in absentia.

WE ESPECIALLY WANT TO THANK OUR FRIENDS AND SUPPORTERS IN EUROPE WHO OPENED THE WAY FOR US TO FILM THE 13 EPISODES OF *SMART TRAVELS*:

London	Out-of-London
Athenaeum Hotel	His Grace the Duke of Marlborough,
Dulwich Picture Gallery	Blenheim Palace, Woodstock,
Tamarind Restaurant	Oxfordshire, UK
Madame Tussaud's Waxworks	Hampton Court Palace
Tate Modern at Bankside	Ashmolean Museum, Oxford
The Science Museum	Mark Allen
Charles Dickens House	Alex Ivey
London Eye	University Church
The Royal Parks	Alice's Shop
	The Trout Inn
	Stonehenge
	Great Hall, Winchester
	www.hants.gov.uk
	Winchester Cathedral
	Jane Austen's House

ACKNOWLEDGMENTS

Copenhagen and Denmark

Lillian Hess
Danish Tourist Board
Wonderful Copenhagen Tourist Office
Danmarks Turistraad
Roskilde Tourist Bureau
Marianne Wirenfeldt Asmussen
Karen Blixen Museum
Nicolai Wirenfeldt Asmussen
Louisiana Museum of Modern Art
Tivoli Gardens
Danish Design Center
Lejre Experimental Center
Viking Ship Museum
Fredericksborg Castle
Kronborg Castle
Radisson SAS Hotel

Amsterdam and The Netherlands

Amsterdam Tourist Board
Albert Holtslag
Rijksmuseum Amsterdam
Anne Frank House
Van Gogh Museum
Museum Amstelkring
Restaurant Puri Mas
Zaanse Schans
Muiderslot
Panorama Mesdag
Madurodam
Koninklijke Porceleyne Fles
In den Porceleyne Winkel

Brussels and Belgium

Liliane Opsomer
Belgian Tourist Office
Brussels Tourist Office
Flanders Tourist Office

In Brussels:
Galler Chocolates
City of Brussels Museum
Theatre Royal de Toone
Le Falstaff Restaurant
Royal Museum of Fine Arts
Musical Instruments Museum
Cathedrale des St. Michel et Ste. Gudule

Atomium
Belgian Comic Strip Center
Royal Museum for Central Africa
Hotel Amigo

In Bruges:
Monasterium de Wijngaard
Begijnhof
Gruuthuse Museum
Kantcentrum
Cathedral of Our Lady

Paris

Stephanie Levin
Musée Rodin
Musée d'Orsay
Notre Dame de Paris
St. Severin
Galeries Lafayette
Café de Flore
Les Bookinistes Restaurant
    bookinistes@guysavoy.com
Brasserie "L'Escurial" 28, rue de Turenne
Jo Goldberg
Le Coude Fou Wine Bar – 12, rue du
    Bourg-Tibourg
RATP & SNCF Paris
G. Robineau Boulangers – 24, rue Cler

Provence

The Minneapolis Institute of Arts
Vacationsfrance.com
Duncan Erskine
Madame Vardi
Atelier Paul Cezanne
Aix Office du Tourisme
    aixtour@pacwan.mm-soft.fr
Abbaye Notre-Dame de Senanque
    ndsenanque@aol.com
La Maison
    www.lamaison-a-bournissac.com
Chez Bru Restaurant
    sbru@club-internet.fr
Arles Service Patrimonie

Venice

Basilica di San Marco
Santa Maria Gloriosa dei Frari
Gallerie dell'Accademia
Italian Tourist Office – John
Hotel Cipriani **info@hotelcipriani.it**
Orient Express Hotels – Patricia Harper
Ca' Macana Mask Shop
www.maskvenice.com
Cantinone Storico, Dorsoduro 660, S. Vio
Cantina do Mori, S. Polo 429, Rialto
I Lirici glassworks, Murano
www.ilirici.com
Vetreria ai Doge snc
www.dogimuranoglass.com
Marco d'Appolonia, gondolier

Genoa and the Italian Riviera

Liguria Regional Tourist Office
Pisa Tourist Office
Dr. Roberto Stubinski
Palazzo Reale
Restaurant Rosa, Camogli
Cattedrale di San Lorenzo
Hotel Tiguillio, Rapallo
Hotel Il Giardino, Pisa
Hotel Columbus, Genoa

Italian Hill Towns

Basilica di San Francesco
Siena Tourism Office – Donatella Grilli
Siena Goose Contrada
Castello Banfi
Elizabeth Koenig Pagliantini
Livio Zazzeri – Pienza Cheese Palio
Leo Grilli
Duomo of Siena
Orvieto Tourism Office
Duomo of Orvieto
Museo Claudio Faina
Giuseppe della Fina

Florence

Villa San Michele
Orient Express Hotels, Patricia Harper

Soprintendenza per I Beni Artistici e
    Storici
Villa Poggio a Caiano
Santa Maria Novella
Giotto's Tower
Museo Leonardo da Vinci
Artimino Cantina
Il Viniseo
Hotel Torre Guelfa
Anna
Pitti Mosaici
La Baruciola Trattoria

Rome

Paulo G. and his family
Vicariato di Roma
Pontificio Consiglio delle Comunicazioni
    Sociali
Soprintendenza per I Beni Artistici e
    Storici di Roma
Enoteca al Parlamento, Via dei Prefetti, 15
Pizzeria al Leoncino, Via del Leoncino, 28
Pizzeria Rustica "da Pasquale" Via dei
    Prefetti, 34/a
Zio Ciro Café
Polvere di Tempo, Via del Moro, 59
Giolitti Gelateria

Naples and the Amalfi Coast

Museo Cappella Sansevero
Max Melchiorre
Paestum
Hotel Minerva, Sorrento
Museo Archeologico Nazionale
Pompeii Archeological Excavations
Gran Caffe Gambrinus
Santa Chiara

Index

Belgium, 51
- Bruges, 55
  - Beguinage, 56
  - Cathedral of Our Lady, 56
  - Gruuthuse Museum, 56
  - Markt, 56
- Brussels, 51
  - Atomium, 54
  - Cathedral, 54
  - Comic Strip Center, 54
    - Herge, 54
    - Tin Tin, 54
  - Grand Place, 52
  - Hotel Amigo, 57
  - Le Falstaff, 57
  - Lower Town, 55
  - Manneken Pis, 52
  - Musical Instruments Museum, 53
  - Royal Museum for Central Africa, 55
    - Leopold II, 55
  - Royal Museum of Fine Arts, 53
    - David, Jacques-Louis, 53
  - Theatre Royal de Toone, 52
  - Upper Town, 55

Cameras Abroad, Using, 89

Denmark, 33
- Andersen, Hans Christian, 33, 34
- Copenhagen, 33
  - Amalienburg Square, 35
  - Canal Boats, 34
  - Copenhagen Cards, 36
  - Dansk Design Center, 35
  - Marmokirken, 34
  - Nyhavn, 34
  - Royal Library, 35
  - Stroget, 34
  - The Little Mermaid, 34
  - Tivoli, 33
  - Town Hall Square, 34
    - World Clock, 34
  - Dragor, 35
  - Helsingor, 38
    - Kronborg Castle, 38
  - Hillerod, 37
    - Fredericksborg Castle, 37
  - Lejre Experimental Center, 36
  - Louisiana Museum of Modern Art, 38
  - North Sealand, 36
    - Klampenborg, 36
  - Restaurant Jacobsen, 38
  - Roskilde, 36
    - Viking Ship Museum, 36
  - Rungstedlund, 37
    - Isak Dinesen, 37
    - Karen Blixen, 37

Family Travel, 46

Florence, 101
- Accademia, 103
  - David, 103
  - The Slaves, 103
- Artimino, 108
- Baptistery, 104
  - Gates of Paradise, 105
  - Ghilberti, 104
- Bargello, 102
  - Donatello, 102
    - Donatello's David, 103
- Duomo, 104
  - Bell Tower, 104
  - Brunelleschi, 104
  - Giotto, 104
- Fiesole, 108
- La Baruciola, 108
- Markets, 102
  - Mercato Centrale, 102
  - Mercato Nuovo, 102
- Medici Family, 102

Lorenzo de Medici, 102
Museo dell' Opera del Duomo, 104
Museo Leonardo da Vinci, 108
Oltrarno, 104
    Bartolozzi and Maioli, 105
    Pitti Mosaics, 105
    Ponte Vecchio, 104
Piazza San Spirito, 108
Santa Maria Novella, 105
    Polyptych, 106
    Trinity, 106
Savonarola, 107
Taverna del Bronzino, 108
Uffizi, 106
    Adoration of the Magi, 107
    Botticelli, 107
    Leonardo da Vinci, 107
    Madonna di Ognissanti, 107
Via Tournabuoni, 102
Villa Poggio a Caiano, 107
Villa San Michele Hotel, 108
Vinci, 108
    Museo Leonardo da Vinci, 108
Vinesio, 108

Hill Towns of Italy, 93
Assisi, 97
    Basilica di San Francesco, 97
    St. Francis, 97
Etruscans, 96
Gubbio, 98
Istituto Santissimo Salvatore, 99
Montalcino, 95
    Abbey of Sant' Antimo, 95
    Brunello, 95
    Castello Banfi, 95, 99
Orvieto, 95
    Duomo, 96
    Hotel Maitani, 96, 99
    Maitani, Lorenzo 96
    Museo Claudio Faina, 96
    Volsinii, 96
Park Hotel ai Cappuccini, 99
Pitigliano, 96
San Gimignano, 93
    Ardinghelli, 93
    Salvucci, 93
Siena, 94
    Duomo, 95
    Palazzo Pubblico, 95
    Palio, 94

Torre di Mangia, 95
Via Bianchi di Sopra, 95
Via Di Citta, 95
Sovana, 96
    Tomba della Sirena, 97
    Tomba Ildebranda, 97
Val D'Orcia, 95

Italian Riviera, 85
Camogli, 91
    Ristorante Rosa, 91
Cinque Terre, 87
    Corniglia, 88
    Hotel Cinque Terre, 92
    Manarola, 88
    Monterosso al Mare, 87
    Riomaggiore, 88
    Vernazza, 88
Genoa, 85
    Anthony Van Dyck, 86
    Cattedrale di San Lorenzo, 86
    Chapel of John the Baptist, 86
    Christopher Columbus, 85
    Largo della Zecca, 85
    Palazzo Reale, 86
    Via Garibaldi, 86
Pisa, 90
    Baptistery, 91
        Naked Hercules, 91
        Pisano, Nicola, 91
    Duomo, 90
    Hotel di Stefano, 92
    Leaning Tower, 90
Portofino, 86
    Hotel Splendido, 92
    Splendido Mare, 91

Italy
Amalfi Coast, 121
Capri, 120
    Piazza Umberto, 123
    Villa Helios, 122
Etruscans, 96
Focaccia al Formaggio, 91
Limoncello, 120
Mozzarella di Bufalo, 122
Paestum, 121
Phlegrean Fields, 120
Pompeii, 119
    House of Faun, 118
    Vesuvius, 119

Positano, 122
Renaissance, 101
Ristorante, 77
Sorrento, 120
Tavola Calda, 77
Trattoria, 77
Tiramisu, 82

London, 15
Athenaeum Hotel, The, 24, 25
Beatles, The, 17
　3 Abbey Road, 17
British Airways London Eye, 16
British Museum, The 20
Brown's Hotel, 24
Buckingham Palace, 16
Charles Dickens, 17
　48 Doughty Street, 17
Claridge's, 23
Covent Garden, 18
Dorchester, The 24
Dulwich Picture Gallery, 21
Harrod's, 21
Holmes, Sherlock, 17
　221b Baker Street, 17
Hyde Park, 21
　Serpentine Lake, 21
　Speaker's Corner, 21
Madame Tussaud's Waxworks, 21
　Chamber of Horrors, 21
Parliament, Houses of, 20
　Big Ben, 21
Picasso, Pablo, 17
Ritz, The 24
Science Museum, The 20
St. Paul's Cathedral, 16
Tamarind Restaurant, 22
Tate Modern, The 17
Thames River, 15
Theater, 18
Tower of London, 16
Trafalgar Square, 15
Tube, The 16

Medical Emergencies Abroad, 129

Naples, 117
Archaelogical Museum, National, 118
Caffe Gambrinus, 122
Cappella Sansevero, 117
San Gennaro, 118

Hotel Minerva, 123
Santa Chiara, 118

Netherlands, 41
Amsterdam, 41
　Amstelkring, 44
　Anne Frank House, 43
　Dam Square, 41
　Jordaan Neighborhood, 42
　Red Light District, 43
　Rijksmuseum, 42
　van Gogh Museum, 43
　Vincent van Gogh, 43
　Westerkerk, 43
Delft, 48
Hague, The 45
Madurodam, 48
Mesdag, 46
Muiderslot, 44
Puri Mas Restaurant, 48
Rijsttafel, 48
Vermeer, Johannes, 42
Windmills, 44
Zaanse Schans, 44

Out of London, 27
Abingdon, 29
Blenheim Palace, 29
Carroll, Lewis, 28
Cricket, 28
Hampton Court, 27
King Arthur, 30
Magdalen Bridge, 32
Marlborough, Duke of, 29
Oxford, 28
　Carfax Tower, 28
　Christ Church, 28
　Eastgate Hotel, 32
　Magdalen College, 28
　The Bear, 32
Stonehenge, 30
Vale of White Horse, 29
Wantage, 30
Winchester, 30
　Jane Austen, 31
Woodstock, 29

Paris, 59
Café de Flore, 65
Eiffel Tower, 62
Impressionism, 63

Latin Quarter, 60
Le Coude Fou, 66
Les Bookinistes, 65
Les Invalides, 63
Louvre, The 63
Luxembourg Palace, 62
Marais, 64
    Place des Vosges, 64
Markets, 62
Metro, 65
Montmartre, 63
    Lapin Agile, 63
    Place de Tertre, 63
Musée d'Orsay, 63
Notre Dame, 60
Pompidou Center, 61
    Stravinsky Fountain, 61
Ritz Hotel, The, 64
Rodin Museum, 30
Rue Cler, 65
Shopping, 64
    Galeries Lafayette, 64
    Place Vendôme, 64
St. Severin, 61
Tuileries, 62

Phoning Home From Abroad, 125

Provence, 67
Aix en Provence, 71
    Cours Mirabeau, 71
    Paul Cézanne, 72
Arles, 69
    Café de la Nuit, 72
Avignon, 69
    Abbey of Senanque, 70
    Luberon, 70
    Papal Palace, 69
    Place de l'Horloge, 70
    Pont St. Benezet, 69
Bonnieux, 71
Borie, 70
Cassis, 72
Domaine de Bournissac, 75
Eygalieres, 68
    St. Sixte Chapel, 69
    Chez Bru, 69, 72
Festivals, 69
Gites, 75
Glanum, 68
    Triumphal Arc, 68

Lavender, 70
Les Arenes, 69
    St. Trophime, 69
Pont Julien, 71
Roussillon, 70
St.-Remy-de-Provence, 67
    La Maison, 73
    Vincent van Gogh, 68
Truffles, 72
Walking Trails, 71

Rome, 109
Baths of Caracalla, 111
Campo dei Fiori, 111
Centro Storico, 111
    Pantheon, 111
    Piazza della Rotunda, 111
Coliseum, 110
Enoteca al Parlamento, 114
Fontana delle Tartarughe, 111
Istituto San Giuseppe, 115
Palatine Hill, 110
Palazzo Farnese, 113
Piazza di Spagna, 113
Piazza Navona, 113
Pizzeria al Leoncino, 114
Pizzeria da Pasquale, 114
San Clemente, 111
Teatro di Marcello, 111
Trastevere, 113
    Polvere di Tempo, 113
    Santa Maria in Trastevere, 113
Vatican City, 112
    St. Peter's Basilica, 112
    Sistine Chapel, 113
    Vatican Museum, 113
Via del Corso, 113
    Spanish Steps, 113
    Via Condotti, 113
Via Sacra, 109
    Temple of Vesta, 110

Venice, 77
Burano, 81
Cannaregio, 80
    Madonna dell'Orto, 80
    San Polo, 80
Ca Macana Mask Shop, 82
Cantinone Storico, 82
Casa Cardinal Pizza, 82
Cipriani Hotel, 82

Do Mori, 80
   Chiesa dei Frari, 80
      Assumption of the Virgin, 80
      Triptych, 81
   Do Mori Wine Bar, 82
Dorsoduro, 80
   Accademia, 80
   Campo Santa Margerita, 80
   Ponte di Pugni, 80
   Zattere, 80
Erberia, 79
Gondola, 83
Grand Canal, 78
Mercerie, 79
Murano, 81
Palaces, 82
Pesceria, 79
Piazza San Marco, 78
   Basilica, 78
   Campanile, 78
   Saint Mark, 78
Rialto Bridge, 79
Sumptuary Laws, 79
Torcello, 81
Traghetto, 80
Vaporetto, 80

Web sites, 137

Your Notes

NOTES